Bread, rusks and muffins

Bread, rusks and muffins

Carmen Niehaus

Human & Rousseau
Cape Town ■ Pretoria ■ Johannesburg

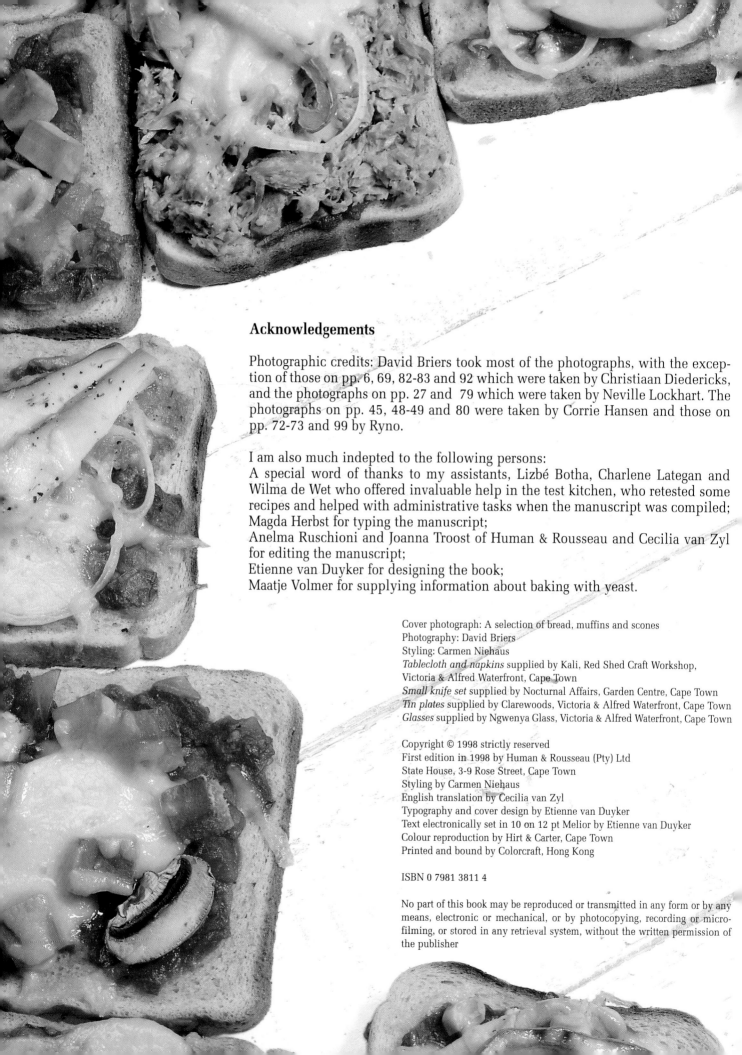

Acknowledgements

Photographic credits: David Briers took most of the photographs, with the exception of those on pp. 6, 69, 82-83 and 92 which were taken by Christiaan Diedericks, and the photographs on pp. 27 and 79 which were taken by Neville Lockhart. The photographs on pp. 45, 48-49 and 80 were taken by Corrie Hansen and those on pp. 72-73 and 99 by Ryno.

I am also much indepted to the following persons:
A special word of thanks to my assistants, Lizbé Botha, Charlene Lategan and Wilma de Wet who offered invaluable help in the test kitchen, who retested some recipes and helped with administrative tasks when the manuscript was compiled;
Magda Herbst for typing the manuscript;
Anelma Ruschioni and Joanna Troost of Human & Rousseau and Cecilia van Zyl for editing the manuscript;
Etienne van Duyker for designing the book;
Maatje Volmer for supplying information about baking with yeast.

Cover photograph: A selection of bread, muffins and scones
Photography: David Briers
Styling: Carmen Niehaus
Tablecloth and napkins supplied by Kali, Red Shed Craft Workshop, Victoria & Alfred Waterfront, Cape Town
Small knife set supplied by Nocturnal Affairs, Garden Centre, Cape Town
Tin plates supplied by Clarewoods, Victoria & Alfred Waterfront, Cape Town
Glasses supplied by Ngwenya Glass, Victoria & Alfred Waterfront, Cape Town

Copyright © 1998 strictly reserved
First edition in 1998 by Human & Rousseau (Pty) Ltd
State House, 3-9 Rose Street, Cape Town
Styling by Carmen Niehaus
English translation by Cecilia van Zyl
Typography and cover design by Etienne van Duyker
Text electronically set in 10 on 12 pt Melior by Etienne van Duyker
Colour reproduction by Hirt & Carter, Cape Town
Printed and bound by Colorcraft, Hong Kong

ISBN 0 7981 3811 4

Contents

Bountiful bread

I love bread, probably because my mother used to spoil us as children with the most heavenly loaves which she used to make with potato yeast. Served fresh from the oven with farm butter and her green fig or apricot jam, it was food fit for a king, especially when we arrived home from boarding school on Friday afternoons, absolutely starving.

We still bake bread at home, but these days we use instant yeast and resort to quick recipes requiring mixing instead of time-consuming kneading. Bread is delicious on its own, spread simply with butter and jam. But there are numerous other ways to serve bread. In this chapter we've included recipes for a garlic ring loaf, a loaf with an onion and cheese topping, potbread and sweet loaves to enjoy with tea or coffee. For those who are a bit hesitant about experimenting with the yeast loaves, we've included a number of quick alternatives such as beer, garlic or mealie loaves. And last but not least we've included recipes for delectable jams, marmalades and other spreads.

Quick bread recipes

Cheese and bacon loaf

Sissy Erasmus of Heidelberg was given this recipe by her English grandmother, and it became a regular Friday supper-time treat.

- 250 ml (1 c) self-raising flour
- pinch salt
- 10 ml (2 t) butter
- 200 ml (⅘ c) grated Cheddar cheese
- 8 rashers streaky bacon, fried and finely chopped
- 150 ml (⅗ c) milk
- 15 ml (1 T) tomato sauce
- 15 ml (1 T) Worcester sauce

Preheat the oven to 200 °C (400 °F). Spray a baking sheet with nonstick spray or grease well with butter or margarine.

Sift together the flour and salt and rub in the butter with your fingertips until the mixture resembles bread-crumbs. Add the cheese and bacon, mixing lightly.

Mix the milk, tomato and Worcester sauces and add to the dry ingredients. Mix lightly until just blended and shape into a circle on the baking sheet. Bake for 20-25 minutes or until done.

Serve hot with butter and cheese.

Serves 3-4.

Cheese and bacon loaf

Garlic loaf

The addition of a packet of garlic steak marinade gives this loaf its subtle garlic aroma. The recipe was sent in by Mrs Dukie Jacobs of Scottburgh.

- 500 g self-raising flour
- 500 ml (2 c) buttermilk
- 1 packet (16 g) garlic steak marinade

Preheat the oven to 180 °C (350 °F). Grease a fairly small loaf tin with butter or margarine, or spray with nonstick spray.

Place all the ingredients in a mixing bowl and mix well to form a soft dough. Turn into the prepared tin and bake about 1 hour or until a testing skewer comes out clean when inserted into the centre of the loaf.

Serve hot with butter.

Makes 1 small loaf.

Handy hints

- Lining the loaf tin: place the loaf tin on a sheet of wax paper and trace the outline of the base. Cut out. Grease the tin and place the cut out paper in the bottom of the tin.
- Lightly mix the liquid and dry ingredients until just blended and moist. Do not overmix as this forms air bubbles in the bread.
- Slice the loaves when completely cooled, or the slices will dry out quickly.

Batter bread with sun-dried tomatoes

Miss L. Sanders of Waverley, Johannesburg, adds extra interest to the usual batter bread made with self-raising flour and buttermilk by adding sun-dried tomatoes. She tops the loaf with onion rings and Cheddar cheese. We used sun-dried tomatoes in oil. If you can find only dried tomatoes, soak them in boiling water until soft, drain and use.

- 950 ml (3⅘ c) self-raising flour
- pinch salt
- 10 ml (2 t) mixed dried herbs
- 1 small onion, finely chopped
- 1 chive, finely chopped
- 100 g sun-dried tomatoes in oil, well drained and finely chopped
- 125 ml (½ c) grated Cheddar cheese
- 1 container (500 ml) buttermilk
- extra cheese and onion rings for sprinkling on top

Preheat the oven to 180 °C (350 °F). Spray a 29 x 11 x 7-cm loaf tin with nonstick spray or grease well with butter or margarine.

Sift the self-raising flour and salt together in a large mixing bowl. Add the mixed herbs, onion, chive, sun-dried tomatoes and Cheddar cheese. Mix well.

Add the buttermilk, mixing lightly with a wooden spoon until just blended. Turn into the prepared loaf tin, spreading evenly. Bake for 1 hour, covering with aluminium foil after 30 minutes. Switch off the oven at the end of the baking time and leave the bread in the oven for another 15 minutes without removing the aluminium foil.

Remove the aluminium foil and sprinkle the extra cheese and onion rings on top. Switch on the oven grill and grill the top of the loaf for a few seconds until the cheese has melted.

Remove from the oven, cool slightly and turn out onto a wire rack.

Serve lukewarm or cold with butter.

Makes 1 medium loaf.

Best beer bread

Beer bread is an old favourite to serve with a braai. Here are a few delicious variations which will make your beer bread taste different every time:

- 500 g self-raising flour
- 5 ml (1 t) salt
- 1 can (340 ml) beer

Preheat the oven to 180 °C (350 °F). Grease a 1,2-litre loaf tin with butter or margarine, or spray with non-stick spray.

Sift the self-raising flour and salt together. Add the beer and mix to form a soft manageable dough. (If the mixture is too stiff, add a little water.) Turn into the prepared tin and bake for about 1 hour or until a testing skewer comes out clean when inserted into the centre of the loaf. Cool slightly in the tin before turning out onto a wire rack.

Serve hot or cold or with butter and cheese. (The bread will have a coarse crust.)

Makes 1 medium loaf.

■ Variations
Add any of the following variations to the basic mixture, mix well and follow the instructions in the basic recipe.

■ Variation 1
250 g bacon, crisply fried and finely chopped
1 green pepper, coarsely chopped and sautéed until soft, or
50 ml (⅕ c) parsley, finely chopped
1 onion, finely chopped and sautéed until soft

■ Variation 2
1 can (410 g) whole-kernel sweetcorn, drained
100 g (250 ml) mature Cheddar cheese, grated

■ Variation 3
9 fresh cloves garlic, crushed
50 ml (⅕ c) parsley, finely chopped

■ Variation 4
Follow the instructions for the basic recipe and turn the mixture into a greased 24-cm cake tin. Sprinkle with 125 ml (½ c) crushed wheat or even sesame and poppy seeds. Bake as described in the basic recipe.

Batter bread with sun-dried tomatoes

Mealie-meal loaf

The sage imparts a unique flavour to this mealie-meal loaf.

- 375 ml (1½ c) milk
- 375 ml (1½ c) mealie meal
- 50 g butter
- 3 extra-large eggs, whisked
- 250 ml (1 c) cake flour
- 15 ml (1 T) baking powder
- 25 ml (5 t) sugar
- 5 ml (1 t) salt
- 7 ml (1½ t) dried sage

Preheat the oven to 200 °C (400 °F). Grease a medium loaf tin with butter or margarine, or spray with non-stick spray.

Bring the milk to the boil and sprinkle with the mealie meal. Add the butter and mix well. Cool and stir in the whisked eggs.

Sift the remaining ingredients together and add to the mealie-meal mixture. Mix well and turn into the tin. Bake for approximately 40 minutes or until the crust is golden brown and the bread done. Turn out onto a wire rack.

Serve hot or cold with butter.

Makes 1 medium loaf.

Olive loaf with sun-dried tomatoes

This loaf has a wonderful Mediterranean flavour.

- 400 ml (1⅗ c) self-raising flour
- 10 ml (2 t) dried rosemary
- pinch salt
- 75 g cold butter
- ½ container (25 g) sun-dried tomatoes in oil, drained and finely chopped
- 50 g green olives, finely chopped
- 1 egg
- 150 ml (⅗ c) milk
- 30 ml (2 T) olive oil
- 5 ml (1 t) coarse sea salt

Preheat the oven to 180 °C (350 °F). Spray a 22 x 11 x 7-cm loaf tin with nonstick spray or grease well with butter or margarine. Line the base with wax paper.

Combine the self-raising flour, rosemary and salt. Grate the butter into the dry ingredients and rub in with your fingertips until the mixture resembles bread-crumbs. Add the tomatoes and olives and mix.

Whisk the egg and milk together and add. Mix and turn into the prepared loaf tin, spreading it evenly. Pour the olive oil on top and sprinkle with coarse sea salt.

Bake for 35-40 minutes or until a testing skewer comes out clean when inserted into the centre of the loaf. Turn out onto a wire rack to cool.

Makes 1 medium loaf.

Cheese bread

Her husband loves this bread which is quick and easy to make, says Mrs Patricia Cilliers of Klerksdorp.

- 500 g self-raising flour
- 2 ml (½ t) salt
- 3 ml (generous ½ t) mustard powder
- 1 ml (¼ t) cayenne pepper
- 500 ml (2 c) buttermilk
- 750 ml (3 c) grated Cheddar cheese

Preheat the oven to 180 °C (350 °F). Grease a 23 x 13 x 7-cm loaf tin with butter or margarine, or spray with nonstick spray.

Sift the dry ingredients together and add the butter-milk and Cheddar cheese. Mix well and turn into the loaf tin. Bake for 50-60 minutes or until a testing skewer comes out clean when inserted into the centre of the loaf.

Makes 1 medium loaf.

Cheese loaf with walnuts

A delectable savoury loaf.

- 400 ml (1⅗ c) self-raising flour
- 7 ml (1½ t) mustard powder
- pinch salt
- 50 g cold butter
- 50 g walnuts, finely chopped
- 45 ml (3 T) finely chopped chives
- 250 ml (1 c) grated Cheddar cheese
- 1 egg
- 150 ml (⅗ c) milk

From left to right: Fruit and almond loaf with honey (p. 26), Lemon loaf with caraway seeds (p. 28), Apple loaf with hazelnuts (p. 29), Olive loaf with sun-dried tomatoes and Cheese loaf with walnuts

Preheat the oven to 180 °C (350 °F). Spray a 22 x 11 x 7-cm loaf tin with nonstick spray or grease with butter or margarine. Line the base with wax paper.

Sift together the self-raising flour, mustard powder and salt. Grate the butter into the dry ingredients and rub in with your fingertips until the mixture resembles breadcrumbs. Add the walnuts, chives and a third of the cheese and mix. Whisk the egg and milk together and add to the flour mixture.

Mix. Turn the mixture into the prepared loaf tin, spreading evenly. Bake for 30 minutes before sprinkling with the remaining cheese. Bake for another 10 minutes or until a testing skewer comes out clean when inserted into the centre of the loaf.

Turn out onto a wire rack to cool.

Makes 1 medium loaf.

Bread that requires no kneading

The Barnyard's whole-wheat seed bread

Their bread is in great demand, says Lisa Dondré, owner of the Barnyard farmstall in Tokai, near Cape Town, and this whole-wheat loaf is always first to go. The dough requires no kneading.

■ 1 kg white bread flour
■ 5 x 250 ml plus 180 ml (5¾ c) whole-wheat flour
■ 50 ml (⅕ c) brown sugar
■ 2 packets (10 g each) instant yeast
■ 125 ml (½ c) sunflower seeds
■ 250 ml (1 c) oats
■ 15 ml (1 T) salt
■ 45 ml (3 T) oil
■ about 1,5 litres (6 x 250 ml) lukewarm water
■ sesame and poppy seeds for sprinkling on top

Preheat the oven to 180 °C (350 °F). Grease two large and one smaller loaf tin with butter or margarine or spray with nonstick spray.

Place all the ingredients, except the water and sesame and poppy seeds, in a large mixing bowl and mix with about 1,5 litres lukewarm water until the mixture is fairly slack, but does not stick to the sides of the bowl.

Cover with greased plastic wrap and leave to rise for 20 minutes. Turn into the prepared tins, cover and leave to rise again until the dough fills the tins. Sprinkle with the sesame and poppy seeds and bake for 25-35 minutes or until the bread sounds hollow when tapped. Turn out onto a wire rack to cool.

Serve with butter or chicken liver pâté (see recipe, p. 33).

Makes 2 large loaves and 1 small one.

From bottom left, clockwise: The Barnyard's spinach muffins (p. 50), Hummus (p. 33), The Barnyard's whole-wheat seed bread and Chicken liver pâté (p. 33)

Whole-wheat bread

Mrs Annaleen van Zyl of Kleinmond always serves this bread with fish. Although the bread is made with yeast, it requires no kneading.

■ 1 kg whole-wheat flour
■ 5 ml (1 t) salt
■ 1 packet (10 g) instant yeast
■ 125 ml (½ c) oil (optional)
■ 1 litre (4 x 250 ml) lukewarm water

Preheat the oven to 180 °C (350 °F). Spray two 29 x 11 x 8 cm loaf tins with nonstick spray or grease well with butter or margarine.

Combine the whole-wheat flour and salt in a mixing bowl and sprinkle the instant yeast on top. Add the oil and lukewarm water and mix well with a wooden spoon.

Turn the dough mixture into the greased loaf tins. Cover with a greased plastic wrap and leave to rise in a warm place until double in volume.

Bake for about 30-40 minutes or until the bread sounds hollow when tapped. Turn the loaf out onto a wire rack and cool slightly before serving.

Makes 2 medium loaves.

Crushed wheat bread

Mrs M. Beukes of Bonnievale mixes the dough for this bread in a large Tupperware bowl and covers it with a lid. She then places the container on a smaller bowl containing hot tap water. When the dough has risen enough the lid simply pops off, she says.

■ 1 kg white bread flour
■ 200 ml (⅘ c) crushed wheat
■ 10 ml (2 t) salt
■ 1 packet (10 g) instant yeast
■ 30 ml (2 T) oil
■ 4 x 250 ml (4 c) lukewarm water

Preheat the oven to 180 °C (350 °F). Spray two 20 x 10 x 7-cm loaf tins with nonstick spray or grease well with butter or margarine.

Place all the ingredients in a large bowl. Stir until well blended. Cover and leave to rise in a warm place until double in volume (or prepare as Mrs Beukes describes). Turn the dough into the prepared loaf tins and leave to rise for another 20 minutes.

Bake for about 45 minutes or until the bread is done and sounds hollow when tapped underneath.

Makes 2 fairly small loaves.

Whole-wheat yoghurt potbread

Bake this potbread over smouldering coals, writes Mrs N. Vermeulen of Napier. A few coals are packed on top of the lid during baking. We tested the recipe by baking the bread in the oven for about an hour.

- 500 ml (2 c) whole-wheat flour
- 250 ml (1 c) oats
- 125 ml (½ c) bran
- 60 ml (¼ c) wheatgerm
- 10 ml (2 t) bicarbonate of soda
- 5 ml (1 t) salt
- 500 ml (2 c) plain yoghurt
- 30 ml (2 T) oil
- 15 ml (1 T) honey

Preheat the oven to 190 °C (375 °F). Spray a heavy 24-cm flat-bottomed pot with nonstick spray or grease well with butter or margarine.

Combine the whole-wheat flour, oats, bran, wheatgerm, bicarbonate of soda and salt in a mixing bowl. Blend the yoghurt, oil and honey and add to the flour mixture. Mix to form a soft dough.

Turn the dough into the prepared pot. Bake for about 1 hour uncovered or until a testing skewer comes out clean when inserted into the centre of the loaf. Cover the bread with a sheet of aluminium foil if it becomes too dark on top.

Makes a fairly flat potbread.

Potbread on the stove plate

If you have a nonstick Bauer pan, you can prepare this potbread on top of the stove.

- 1 packet (10 g) dry yeast (not instant yeast)
- 5 ml (1 t) melted honey
- 250 ml (1 c) lukewarm water
- 750 ml (3 c) whole-wheat flour
- 5 ml (1 t) salt
- 30 ml (2 T) olive oil
- oil
- sunflower seeds (optional)

Mix the dry yeast and honey with a little lukewarm water and leave until frothy.

Meanwhile mix the water, flour, salt and olive oil in a mixing bowl. Add the yeast mixture and mix with a wooden spoon until the mixture no longer sticks to the sides of the bowl. Cover and rest for about 1 hour in a warm place. Knock back and shape into a round pot loaf.

Brush the Bauer pan with oil and place the bread inside the pot. Sprinkle with sunflower seeds if pre-ferred. Cover and leave to rise until double in volume. Place on the stove plate. Bake for about 1 hour over low heat or until the loaf is done – it will sound hollow when tapped underneath. Turn the bread in the pan so the top faces down. Heat for a further 5 minutes to allow the top to brown lightly.

Serve with butter.

Makes 1 loaf.

Different types of yeast

One can purchase different types of yeast at the supermarket or delicatessen: active dry yeast – a granular yeast one can buy in packets or cans; instant yeast – dry yeast available in packets; compressed or fresh yeast – this comes in cubes; Brewer's yeast – available in cubes, packets or cans. (Brewer's yeast is not used for baking.)

Dry yeast may be substituted in recipes calling for fresh or compressed yeast – 25 g cubed yeast equals 1 packet (10 g) dry yeast.

The various types of yeast are not used in the same way. Instant yeast is added directly to the dry ingredients as it does not need to be reactivated before use. However, all the other types of yeast need to be dissolved in a lukewarm sugar solution to be activated. Remember to adapt the method of the recipe according to the type of yeast used.

Whole-wheat yoghurt potbread (back) and Whole-wheat rye bread and rolls (left and front, p. 16)

Bread and rolls that require kneading

Riverside's white bread

Katy Duikers works at the Gate House, a farmstall on the fruit farm Riverside near Simondium. She bakes this bread herself for visitors. Served with the farm's fresh fruit and home-made jams, it's a meal on its own, says Wilna Rabe, Riverside's gracious hostess. (See recipes for jam on pp. 30-33.)

- 1 kg white bread flour
- 15 ml (1 T) instant yeast
- 10 ml (2 t) salt
- 10 ml (2 t) sugar
- 625 ml (2½ c) lukewarm water

Preheat the oven to 190 °C (375 °F). Grease two medium loaf tins with butter or margarine, or spray with nonstick spray.

Mix the white bread flour, instant yeast, salt and sugar in a mixing bowl. Add enough lukewarm water to form a manageable dough. Knead the dough until smooth and elastic and it no longer sticks to your hands. Cover with greased plastic wrap and leave to rest for about 15 minutes in a warm place. Knock back and shape into two loaves, place in the prepared tins, cover and leave to rise for about 40 minutes until double in volume.

Bake for 35-40 minutes in the centre of the oven until the bread is baked through and sounds hollow when gently tapped on top. Turn the loaves out onto a wire rack and spread the crusts with butter.

Makes 2 medium loaves.

Whole-wheat rye bread

Hannetjie Langenhoven of Great Brak River says her kids don't usually like brown bread, but they love this rye bread.

- 6 x 250 ml (6 c) white bread flour
- 750 ml (3 c) whole-wheat flour
- 500 ml (2 c) rye flour
- 250 ml (1 c) cracked wheat
- 10 ml (2 t) salt
- 1 packet (10 g) instant yeast
- 20 ml (4 t) molasses or brown sugar
- 125 g margarine
- 800-900 ml (3⅕-3⅗ c) lukewarm water

Preheat the oven to 190 °C (375 °F). Spray a 22 x 11 x 7-cm loaf tin and baking sheet with nonstick spray or grease well with butter or margarine.

Combine the flours, wheat and salt. Add the instant yeast and molasses. Rub in the margarine with your fingertips until well blended. Add enough lukewarm water to make a manageable dough. Knead well until the dough is smooth and elastic and no longer sticks to your hands.

Cover with greased plastic wrap and rest for about 10 minutes. Knock back and shape into a loaf large enough to fill the tin halfway. Shape the remaining dough into 10 round rolls. Arrange on the baking sheet, spacing far apart. Cover with greased plastic wrap and leave to rise until double in volume.

Bake the bread for about 30-40 minutes or until done and a testing skewer comes out clean when inserted into the centre of the loaf. Bake the rolls for about 20 minutes or until done.

Makes a small loaf and 10 rolls.

Overnight rolls

Mix the dough the night before and leave in the fridge to rise overnight. The rolls will be ready for baking the next morning.

- 7 x 250 ml (7 c) white bread flour
- 10 ml (2 t) salt
- 1 packet (10 g) instant yeast
- 50 ml (⅕ c) melted butter
- 2 extra-large eggs
- 500 ml (2 c) lukewarm milk
- milk for brushing

Combine the bread flour, salt and instant yeast in a large mixing bowl. Add the butter and eggs and mix lightly.

Add small quantities of the lukewarm milk and mix well with your hand to form a soft, manageable dough.

Knead for 10 minutes or until the dough is smooth and elastic and no longer sticks to your hands. Divide the dough in half and shape each half into six balls. Flatten slightly and arrange on a greased baking sheet. Cover with greased plastic wrap and leave in a cool place or in the fridge overnight to rise slowly until double in volume.

Preheat the oven to 220 °C (425 °F). Brush each roll with a little milk and bake for 10-15 minutes or until brown on top.

Serve hot with butter and cheese.

Makes 12 rolls.

Riverside's white bread with Plum, Nectarine and Grape jam (p. 30)

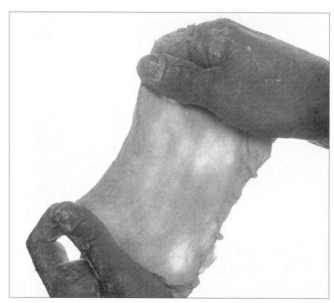

German buns

Hannes Hotarek of Anchor Yeast was recently named the Wheat Board's Baker of the Year. He showed us step by step how to make these rolls. Serve them with coffee for breakfast. All they need is a bit of butter – nothing more.

- 1 kg cake flour
- 2 packets (10 g each) instant yeast
- 600 ml (2⅖ c) lukewarm water
- 17,5 ml (1½ T) salt
- 15 ml (1 T) caramel brown sugar
- 25 ml (5 t) soft margarine

Prepare a sponge dough: Mix 500 g of the cake flour, 1 packet instant yeast and 600 ml lukewarm water in a mixing bowl, cover with plastic wrap and leave for 1 hour in a warm place until the dough is spongy. Add the remaining cake flour and instant yeast, plus the remaining ingredients, mixing well to form a stiff dough (add more cake flour if necessary).

Knead the dough on a floured surface for about 10 minutes or until it is smooth and elastic. Use a press and fold action to incorporate air into the dough (picture 1).

Test if the dough has been sufficiently kneaded by breaking off a small piece and stretching it between your thumb and forefinger until it is transparent but does not break (picture 2).

Cover the dough with a tea towel and leave it to rest for about 10 minutes. Roll the dough into an oblong roll and cut into 10 pieces each weighing about 800 g.

Shape into balls, cover with a tea towel and leave to rest so the dough can 'relax'. Make a slit in each bun with the back of a wooden spoon (picture 3).

Arrange the buns, slit side facing down, on greased baking sheets, cover with a damp tea towel and leave for about 20 minutes. Turn and leave to rise for about another 20 minutes or until double in volume. Brush with water and bake for 10 minutes at 240 °C (475 °F). Reduce the oven temperature to 180 °C (350 °F) and bake for another 10 minutes or until done.

Serve with butter.

Makes about 30 buns.

German buns

Hot cross buns

Treat your family and friends to home-made hot cross buns.

DOUGH
- 4 x 250 ml (4 c) cake flour
- 5 ml (1 t) salt
- 60 ml (¼ c) sugar
- 3 ml (generous ½ t) mixed dried spice
- 3 ml (generous ½ t) nutmeg
- 5 ml (1 t) cinnamon
- 1 packet (10 g) instant yeast
- 60 g (60 ml) margarine
- 150 ml (⅗ c) hot milk
- 1 large egg, whisked
- 125 ml (½ c) lukewarm water
- 250 ml (1 c) dried fruitcake mix

TOPPING
- 250 ml (1 c) cake flour
- 1 ml (¼ t) salt
- 50 ml (⅕ c) oil
- 150 ml (⅗ c) milk
- 1 large egg, whisked
- sugar water for glazing

Preheat the oven to 200 °C (400 °F). Grease a baking sheet with butter or margarine, or spray with nonstick spray.

■ DOUGH: Sift the cake flour, salt, sugar, mixed spice, nutmeg and cinnamon together. Add the instant yeast and mix.

Melt the margarine in the hot milk and cool slightly. Add the milk mixture and whisked egg to the dry ingredients, adding enough lukewarm water to form a soft dough. Knead the dough well for about 15 minutes

Hot cross buns

until smooth and elastic and it no longer sticks to your hands. Place on a lightly floured surface, cover with greased plastic wrap and leave to rest for 15 minutes.

Knock back the dough and work in the dried fruit-cake mix while kneading. Divide the dough into 18 equal balls, shape into buns and place on the prepared baking sheet. Cover with greased plastic and leave to rise in a warm place until double in volume, about 25-30 minutes.

■ TOPPING: Mix the flour, salt and oil. Gradually add the milk until the batter is thin enough to pipe, yet firm enough to retain its shape.

Brush the buns with whisked egg and pipe a cross over each bun with the topping batter. Bake for 15-20 minutes. Glaze with hot sugar water while the buns are still hot.

Makes 18 hot cross buns.

Fancy bread and loaves

Round loaf with cheese and onion topping

Use red onions to make this delicious loaf and serve it straight from the oven.

ONION MIXTURE
■ 45 ml (3 T) butter
■ 450 g red onions, sliced into rings

BASIC BREAD DOUGH
■ 500 ml (2 c) white bread flour
■ 1 ml (¼ t) salt
■ 1 packet (10 g) instant yeast
■ 200 ml (⅘ c) lukewarm water

TOPPING
■ 200 g Tusser's cheese, grated
■ 30 ml (2 T) milk
■ few sprigs fresh rosemary (optional)

Preheat the oven to 200 °C (400 °F). Spray a 20-cm loose-bottomed cake tin with nonstick spray or grease well with butter or margarine.

■ ONION MIXTURE: Heat the butter in a pan and sauté the onions until tender. Remove from the pan and set aside to cool.

■ DOUGH: Combine the flour, salt and instant yeast in a mixing bowl. Add just enough lukewarm water to form a soft, manageable dough. Knead for 10 minutes or until the dough is smooth and elastic and no longer sticks to your hands. Rest for 10 minutes, knock back and shape in a round loaf. Place in the prepared cake tin and cover with greased plastic wrap. Leave to rise in a warm place until double in volume, about 1 hour.

■ TOPPING: Meanwhile mix the cheese and milk with the onions. Remove the plastic wrap and spoon the onion mixture on top of the bread dough. Sprinkle with rosemary if preferred and bake for 30-35 minutes or until the loaf is done. Cool slightly, remove the loaf and place on a serving platter. Serve hot.

Makes 1 large round loaf.

Flat loaf with sun-dried tomatoes

Use the same basic bread recipe as for the round loaf, but add sun-dried tomatoes to the dough. The loaf is topped with cheese and coarse salt.

■ 1 x basic bread dough recipe (see recipe, left)
■ 45 ml (3 T) green pesto sauce (optional)
■ 8 sun-dried tomatoes in oil, drained and finely chopped
■ 30 ml (2 T) olive oil
■ 50 g Tusser's cheese, grated
■ 5 ml (1 t) coarse salt
■ few fresh basil leaves (optional)

Preheat the oven to 200 °C (400 °F). Spray a small, deep baking sheet with nonstick spray or grease well with butter or margarine.

Prepare the bread dough as in the previous recipe, then add the pesto sauce while kneading. Add the sun-dried tomatoes 2 minutes before the end of the 10-minute kneading time. Leave to rest for 10 minutes.

Press the dough onto the prepared baking sheet and cover with a sheet of greased plastic wrap. Leave to rise in a warm place until double in volume, about 1 hour.

Remove the plastic wrap, brush the dough with olive oil and sprinkle with the cheese and salt. Bake for 30 minutes or until brown on top and done.

Sprinkle with basil if preferred. Slice thinly and serve lukewarm. The bread is also delicious lightly toasted.

Makes 1 loaf.

The Barnyard's focaccia (Italian bread)

Customers come from all over to buy this traditional Italian bread at the Barnyard farmstall in Tokai near Cape Town. Ring the changes by kneading sun-dried tomatoes or olives with fried onions and a variety of freshly chopped herbs into the dough. Serve with braaivleis or soup.

- 625 ml (2½ c) white bread flour
- 2 ml (½ t) salt
- 10 ml (2 t) instant yeast
- 210 ml (⅘ c plus 2 t) lukewarm water
- 15 ml (1 T) olive oil
- a mixture of 8-10 sun-dried tomatoes, finely chopped; 1 chopped and fried onion; and 50 ml (¼ c) chopped, fresh herbs
- extra olive oil, chopped herbs and garlic for sprinkling on top

The Barnyard's focaccia (Italian bread)

Preheat the oven to 190 °C (375 °F). Spray two baking sheets with nonstick spray or grease well with butter or margarine.

Sift the flour and salt together into a large bowl. Sprinkle the instant yeast on top. Add the water, olive oil and tomato and herb mixture. Mix well and knead for about 10 minutes until the dough no longer sticks to your hands or the sides of the bowl.

Cover with greased plastic wrap and leave to rise in a warm place until double in volume. Knock back and divide in half. Shape each half into a ball, flatten slightly and make a cross on top of the dough with a knife. Sprinkle with a little olive oil, chopped herbs and garlic. Cover and leave to rise again for about 30 minutes until double in volume.

Bake for 20-25 minutes or until done.
Makes 2 loaves.

Garlic ring

Every time she makes this garlic ring for a braai, guests ask her for a copy of the recipe, writes Susan Grobler of Blinkpan.

GARLIC SAUCE
- 180 ml (¾ c) melted butter
- 3 cloves garlic, crushed
- 25 ml (5 t) freshly chopped parsley
- 10 ml (2 t) mixed dried herbs

BREAD
- 2 extra-large eggs
- 25 ml (5 t) oil
- 500 ml (2 c) lukewarm water
- 60 ml (¼ c) sugar
- 1 packet (10 g) instant yeast
- 1 clove garlic, crushed
- pinch ginger
- 5 x 250 ml (5 c) cake flour

Preheat the oven to 190 °C (375 °F). Spray two 23-cm loose-bottomed cake tins with nonstick spray or grease well with butter or margarine.

■ GARLIC SAUCE: Mix all the ingredients for the garlic sauce in a saucepan and heat until butter has melted. Cool slightly and set aside.

■ BREAD: Whisk together the eggs, oil, water and sugar. Mix the remaining dry ingredients in 'n large mixing bowl. Add the egg mixture and mix to form a soft dough. Knead for 10 minutes or until the dough is smooth and elastic and no longer sticks to your hands.

Cover with greased plastic wrap and leave to rise in a warm place for 20 minutes. Divide the dough in half and shape each half into 12 uniform balls. Roll each ball in the melted butter mixture and arrange in the

prepared cake tins. Cover with greased plastic wrap and leave to rise until double in volume.

Bake for 35-40 minutes or until done and brown on top. Serve lukewarm with braaied meat or soup.
Makes 2 loaves.

Herbed bread roll

Serve this bread with pasta dishes, braaied meat or soup.

FILLING
- 125 ml (½ c) finely chopped, mixed fresh herbs such as parsley, sage and origanum
- 2 cloves garlic, crushed
- 50 g ground almonds
- 50 g Parmesan cheese, grated
- 150 ml (⅗ c) olive oil
- salt and freshly ground black pepper

BREAD DOUGH
- 5 x 250 ml plus 180 ml (5 c plus ¾ c) white bread flour
- 5 ml (1 t) salt
- 1 packet (10 g) instant yeast
- 450 ml (1⅘ c) lukewarm water
- 1 extra-large egg, whisked

Preheat the oven to 190 °C (375 °F). Spray a large baking sheet with nonstick spray or grease well with butter or margarine.

■ FILLING: Mix the fresh herbs, garlic, almonds and Parmesan cheese in a food processor. Switch on the food processor and pour small quantities of the olive oil through the spout until well blended with the herb mixture. Season with salt and pepper. Chill until needed.

■ BREAD DOUGH: Combine the bread flour, salt and instant yeast in a mixing bowl. Add just enough lukewarm water to form a stiff dough. Knead the dough well until smooth and elastic and until it no longer sticks to your hands, at least 10 minutes. Cover with greased plastic wrap and leave to rest in a warm place for 10 minutes.

Knock the dough back and roll out until about 1 cm thick. Spread with the filling, leaving a 5-cm edge all round. Brush the edge with the whisked egg and roll up the dough. Press the open ends firmly together and place the roll on a baking sheet.

Cover and leave in a warm place to rise, about 20-30 minutes. Brush the top of the roll with whisked egg and bake for about 20-30 minutes or until done.

Slice and serve hot with butter if preferred. Slices of mozzarella cheese and tomato, cottage cheese with ham or salami and gherkins also go well with the bread.
Makes 1 large loaf.

Courgette and olive mini-loaves

These little loaves take only 20 minutes to bake.

COURGETTE MIXTURE
- 200 g courgettes, rinsed and grated
- oil
- 15 ml (1 T) finely chopped fresh origanum
- 15 ml (1 T) finely chopped fresh thyme
- ½ packet (50 g) almond flakes or pine kernels (optional)
- salt and freshly ground black pepper

BREAD DOUGH
- 400 ml (1⅗ c) white bread flour
- 1 ml (¼ t) salt
- 1 packet (10 g) instant yeast
- 25 ml (5 t) melted butter
- 300 ml (1⅕ c) lukewarm milk
- 50 g black olives, halved and stoned
- milk for brushing
- extra pine kernels or almond flakes for sprinkling on top (optional)

Preheat the oven to 200 °C (400 °F). Spray three small baking sheets with nonstick spray or grease well with butter or margarine.
- COURGETTE MIXTURE: Sauté the courgettes in a little oil with the origanum and thyme until just tender but still crisp. Add the almond flakes if preferred and stir-fry until lightly browned. Season with salt and pepper and cool.
- BREAD DOUGH: Combine the white bread flour, salt and instant yeast. Add the butter and lukewarm milk and mix to form a soft, manageable dough. Knead for 10 minutes or until the dough is smooth and elastic and no longer sticks to your hands. Add the courgette mixture while kneading. Add the olives 2 minutes before the end of the kneading time and knead until well mixed. Divide the dough into 3 parts, shaping each part into a flat, round loaf. Cover with greased plastic wrap and leave to rise in a warm place until double in volume, about 1 hour.

Remove the plastic wrap, brush with milk, sprinkle with extra pine kernels or almond flakes and bake for 15-20 minutes or until baked through and golden brown.

Serve lukewarm with butter.
Makes 3 small loaves.

Flat mealie-meal bread

These flat breads originated in Italy and are delicious.

BREAD
- 400 ml (1⅗ c) cake flour
- 400 ml (1⅗ c) mealie meal
- pinch salt
- 10 ml (2 t) instant yeast
- 37,5 ml (2½ T) cooking oil
- 250 ml (1 c) lukewarm water
- 125 ml (½ c) whole-kernel sweetcorn
- 2 tomatoes, skinned and chopped
- 125 ml (½ c) olive oil
- 12,5 ml (2½ t) dried thyme
- 2 cloves garlic, chopped

YOGHURT SAUCE
- 150 ml (⅗ c) plain yoghurt
- 50 g (125 ml) almonds, chopped

Preheat the oven to 190 °C (375 °F). Spray a large baking sheet with nonstick spray or grease well with butter or margarine.
- BREAD: Mix the cake flour, mealie meal, salt and instant yeast together. Add the cooking oil and enough lukewarm water to make a stiff dough. Knead well and leave to rise in a warm place. Halve the dough and roll out each half until flat. Arrange half the sweetcorn on one half of the dough and roll over the dough once more with the rolling pin. Place the chopped tomatoes on the other dough half and sprinkle the remaining sweetcorn on top.

Place the two dough halves on the baking sheet. Mix the olive oil, thyme and garlic and drizzle over the two halves of dough. Leave to rise until double in volume. Bake for about 30 minutes or until done and golden brown on top.
- YOGHURT SAUCE: Mix the yoghurt and almonds and serve with the bread.
Makes 2 flat loaves.

Tea loaves

Dark fruitcake loaves

This amount of batter makes two loaves. Decorate with whole almonds.

FRUIT MIXTURE
- 500 ml (2 c) raisins
- 250 ml (1 c) sultanas
- 500 ml (2 c) currants
- 250 g dates, finely chopped
- 250 g cherries, finely chopped
- 250 g mixed citrus peel
- 125 ml (½ c) brandy

BATTER

- 250 g butter
- 310 ml (1¼ c) soft brown sugar
- 7 extra-large eggs
- grated rind of 1 orange
- grated rind of 1 lemon
- 825 ml (3 c plus 5 T) cake flour
- 7 ml (1½ t) salt
- 5 ml (1 t) nutmeg
- 1-2 packets (100 g each) whole almonds

■ FRUIT MIXTURE: Mix all the fruit and the citrus peel and pour the brandy over. Cover and leave for a few hours or overnight.

Preheat the oven to 150 °C (300 °F). Line two 23 x 11 x 9-cm loaf tins with aluminium foil. Spray with non-stick spray or grease well with butter or margarine.

■ BATTER: Beat the butter until light and creamy. Add small quantities of brown sugar at a time while beating continuously. Add the eggs one by one, beating well after each addition.

Add the orange and lemon rind and mix. Sift in the cake flour, salt and nutmeg and mix well.

Pour the batter over the fruit and mix well. Turn the batter into the prepared loaf tins and arrange the whole almonds on top.

Cover with an aluminium foil lid and bake for 3 hours or until done. The fruit loaves are done when a testing skewer comes out clean when inserted into the centre of the loaves. Cool completely and store in an airtight container.

Makes 2 loaves.

Dark fruitcake loaves

Brown banana loaf

Banana loaves are much healthier made with brown bread flour, writes Theresa Litana of Ndola in Zambia.

- 110 g butter
- 150 ml (⅗ c) caster sugar
- 2 extra-large eggs
- 250 ml (1 c) brown bread flour
- 10 ml (2 t) baking powder
- pinch salt
- 2 ripe bananas, peeled and mashed

Preheat the oven to 180 °C (350 °F). Spray a 22 x 11 x 7-cm loaf tin with nonstick spray or grease well with butter or margarine.

Cream the butter and add small quantities of caster sugar while beating continuously. Add the eggs one by one, beating well after each addition.

Sift the flour, baking powder and salt together and fold into the butter mixture. Add the bran left behind in the sieve to the mixture. Add the bananas and fold in. Turn the mixture into the prepared loaf tin and bake for 30-35 minutes or until the loaf is done and a testing skewer comes out clean when inserted into the centre of the loaf. Cool slightly before turning out onto a wire rack to cool.

Slice and serve with butter.

Makes 1 medium loaf.

Brown ginger loaf

Here's another healthy recipe made with brown bread flour sent in by Theresa Litana of Ndola in Zambia.

- 500 ml (2 c) brown bread flour
- 4 ml (¾ t) salt
- 4 ml (¾ t) bicarbonate of soda
- 4 ml (¾ t) ginger
- 4 ml (¾ t) ground cinnamon
- 110 g butter
- 125 ml (½ c) caster sugar
- 1 extra-large egg
- 125 ml (½ c) golden syrup, slightly heated
- 125 ml (½ c) boiling water

Preheat the oven to 180 °C (350 °F). Spray a 22 x 11 x 7-cm loaf tin with nonstick spray or grease well with butter or margarine.

Sift the flour, salt, bicarbonate of soda, ginger and cinnamon together in a large mixing bowl.

Cream the butter and add small quantities of the caster sugar at a time while beating continuously. Add the egg and golden syrup and beat well. Add dry ingredients, alternating with the boiling water. Mix well.

Turn into the prepared loaf tin and bake for 35-40 min-utes or until the loaf is done and a testing skewer comes out clean when inserted into the centre of the loaf. Cool slightly before turning out onto a wire rack to cool.

Slice and serve with butter.

Makes 1 medium loaf.

Whole-wheat date loaf

Enjoy this loaf fresh from the oven. All it needs is a lit-tle butter, says Farzanah Vorajee of Rosepark, Ladysmith.

- 250 g stoned dates, coarsely chopped or 250 g mixed dried fruit
- 5 ml (1 t) bicarbonate of soda
- 150 ml (⅗ c) boiling water
- 50 g butter or margarine
- 2 extra-large eggs
- 50 ml (⅕ c) golden syrup
- 250 ml (1 c) whole-wheat flour
- 250 ml (1 c) cake flour
- 1 ml (¼ t) salt
- 10 ml (2 t) baking powder

Preheat the oven to 180 °C (350 °F). Spray a 21 x 11 x 6-cm loaf tin with nonstick spray or grease well with butter or margarine.

Place the dates in a bowl and sprinkle the bicarbon-ate of soda on top. Pour over the boiling water and add the butter. Mix until the butter has melted. Cool.

Beat the eggs until thick and light and add the golden syrup, beating until well blended. Add to the date mixture.

Sift the whole-wheat flour, cake flour, salt and bak-ing powder together. Add the bran left behind in the sieve and the date mixture to the flour mixture. Mix well. Turn into the loaf tin, spreading evenly. Bake for 45-60 minutes until golden brown and baked through.

Makes a small loaf.

Fruit and almond loaf with honey

This loaf is made with a layer of sultanas and whole almonds in the centre and is topped with honey.

- 400 ml (1⅗ c) self-raising flour
- 2 ml (½ t) ground cinnamon
- 75 g butter
- 50 g glacé fruit, chopped
- 30 ml (2 T) caster sugar
- 1 egg, whisked
- 80 ml (⅓ c) milk
- 60 ml (4 T) honey
- 50 g sultanas
- 50 g whole almonds
- grated rind of 1 orange

Preheat the oven to 190 °C (375 °F). Spray a 22 x 11 x 7-cm loaf tin with nonstick spray or grease well with butter or margarine and line the bottom with wax paper.

Sift together the self-raising flour and cinnamon. Grate in the butter and rub it in with your fingertips until the mixture resembles breadcrumbs. Add the glacé fruit and caster sugar. Add the whisked egg and milk and mix to form a soft dough.

Turn half the batter into the prepared loaf tin, spreading it evenly. Mix half the honey with the sultanas, almonds and orange rind and spoon on batter in tin, spreading it evenly. Turn remaining batter into tin, spreading it evenly. Pour remaining honey on top.

Bake for 45-50 minutes or until a testing skewer comes out clean when inserted into the centre of the loaf. Cover with a sheet of aluminium foil if the top layer becomes too dark and the loaf is not completely done. Turn out onto a wire rack to cool.

Makes 1 medium loaf.

Brown banana loaf (left) and Brown ginger loaf (right)

Lemon loaf with caraway seeds

The caraway seed imparts a special flavour to this loaf, but even without the loaf still has a beautiful lemon flavour.

- 100 g butter
- 125 ml (½ c) caster sugar
- grated rind and juice of 1 lemon
- 2 eggs, separated
- 300 ml (1⅕ c) self-raising flour
- 15 ml (1 T) caraway seeds
- 30 ml (2 T) caster sugar
- juice of 1 lemon

Preheat the oven to 190 °C (375 °F). Spray a 22 x 11 x 7-cm loaf tin with nonstick spray or grease well with butter or margarine and line the bottom with wax paper.

Cream the butter and caster sugar until light and fluffy. Add the lemon rind, and whisk in the egg yolks one by one.

Sift the self-raising flour and fold into the butter mixture along with the caraway seeds and lemon juice.

Whisk the egg whites until soft peaks are formed and fold into the flour mixture.

Turn the mixture into the prepared loaf tin, spreading it evenly. Bake for 30-35 minutes or until a testing skewer comes out clean when inserted into the centre of the loaf. Turn out onto a wire rack and sprinkle with the 30 ml caster sugar and juice of 1 lemon.

Makes 1 medium loaf.

Carrot fruit loaf

This loaf, packed with fruit, freezes well, writes Rhona Strydom of Algoapark, Port Elizabeth.

- 450 g carrots, grated
- 1 packet (250 g) seedless raisins
- 250 g stoned dates, finely chopped
- grated rind and juice of 1 orange
- 100 g red glacé cherries
- 250 ml (1 c) water
- 250 ml (1 c) sugar
- 250 ml (1 c) oil
- 6 extra-large eggs, whisked
- 4 x 250 ml (4 c) cake flour
- 10 ml (2 t) baking powder
- 10 ml (2 t) bicarbonate of soda
- 5 ml (1 t) salt
- 2 ml (½ t) ground cloves
- 2 ml (½ t) nutmeg
- 15 ml (1 T) ground cinnamon
- 2 ml (½ t) ground ginger

Preheat the oven to 180 °C (350 °F). Grease two 23 x 13 x 7-cm loaf tins with butter or margarine, or spray with nonstick spray.

Place the grated carrots, raisins, dates, orange juice and rind, glacé cherries, water, sugar and oil in a heavy-bottomed saucepan.

Heat slowly until the sugar has dissolved. Stir occasionally. Bring to the boil and simmer slowly for 5 minutes. Remove from the heat and cool.

Add the whisked eggs to the cooled fruit mixture, mixing well. Sift in the dry ingredients and mix well. Turn the mixture into the greased loaf tins and bake for 1 hour or until a testing skewer comes out clean when inserted into the centre of the loaves. (Cover the loaves with aluminium foil if the crusts turn too brown and the loaves are not yet baked through.)

Serve with butter.

Makes 2 medium loaves.

Health fruit loaf

Anna McClelland has been living in Forest Hill, Australia after emigrating a while ago. She uses her Winning Recipes all the time, but is quick to point out that Australians are excellent cooks. To prove it she's sent us this recipe, given to her by her sister-in-law Janet.

- 180 ml (¾ c) coconut
- 180 ml (¾ c) sugar
- 180 ml (¾ c) oats
- 250 ml (1 c) bran
- 375 ml (1½ c) self-raising flour
- 5 ml (1 t) baking powder
- 200 g (330 ml) sultanas
  or shredded dried apricots
  or mixed dried fruit
- 125 ml (½ c) sunflower seeds or
  pumpkin pips or pine kernels
- 2 extra-large eggs, whisked
- 375 ml (2½ c) skimmed milk
- poppy seeds for sprinkling on top

Preheat the oven to 180 °C (350 °F). Spray a 23 x 13 x 7-cm loaf tin with nonstick spray or grease well with butter or margarine.

Combine the dry ingredients. Add sultanas and sunflower seeds and mix well.

Whisk the eggs and skimmed milk until just blended, add to the dry ingredients and mix. Turn mixture into the prepared loaf tin and sprinkle with poppy seeds.

Bake for about 1 hour or until a testing skewer comes out clean when inserted into the centre of the loaf. Cool slightly before turning out onto a wire rack. Serve with butter.

Makes a medium loaf.

Apple loaf with hazelnuts

Hazelnuts give this tasty apple loaf a deliciously coarse texture.

- 400 ml (1⅗ c) self-raising flour
- 5 ml (1 t) baking powder
- 2 ml (½ t) mixed spice
- 50 g seedless raisins
- 125 ml (½ c) caramel brown sugar
- 50 g hazelnuts, finely chopped
- 225 g Granny Smith apples, peeled, cored and finely chopped
- 2 eggs
- 50 g butter, melted
- 75 ml (5 T) apple juice

Preheat the oven to 180 °C (350 °F). Spray a 23 x 13 x 7-cm loaf tin with nonstick spray or grease well with butter or margarine and line the bottom with wax paper.

Sift the self-raising flour, baking powder and spices together and add the raisins, sugar, nuts and apples. Mix.

Beat the eggs, melted butter and apple juice together and add to the dry ingredients. Turn the mixture into the prepared loaf tin, spreading it evenly.

Bake for about 1¼-1½ hours or until a testing skewer comes out clean when inserted into the centre of the loaf. Turn out onto a wire rack to cool completely.

Makes 1 medium loaf.

Carrot fruit loaf

Jams and spreads

Plum or nectarine jam

For 20 years Miemie Abrahams has been the mainstay in the kitchen at Riverside farm near Simondium. Thanks to her the shelves are always well stocked with a variety of jams. Use the orchard run – top-quality fruit that's discarded – to make jam.

- 2 kg plums or nectarines, stoned but with skin and diced (reserve the stones)
- 500 ml (2 c) water
- 2 kg sugar
- 15 ml (1 T) lemon juice
- 1 piece crushed fresh ginger

Boil the fruit and water until the fruit is just tender – the back of a match must easily pierce the skin of the fruit. Add the stones to the mixture.

Remove the saucepan from the heat. Remove the stones and add the sugar. Stir well and leave until all the sugar has dissolved. Add the lemon juice and ginger, return the saucepan to the heat and boil slowly for about 45 minutes until the jam is ready.

Scoop off the scum that forms on top of the mixture and stir occasionally. (To test if the jam is ready, Wilna, Riverside's hostess, suggests the following: Spoon a little of the jam onto a saucer. If the jam feels like honey – it feels as if the spoon slides over the saucer – the jam is ready.)

Spoon the jam into clean, sterilised jars and store in a cool place.

Enough for about 3-4 honey jars.

Grape jam

Grape jam remains an old favourite.

- 2 kg grapes, halved and seeds removed
- 250 ml (1 c) water
- 2 kg sugar (if using hanepoot grapes, use 750 g sugar for every 1 kg grapes)
- lemon juice (15 ml [1 T] per 1 kg fruit)

Boil the grapes in the water until just tender. Arrange the grapes and sugar in layers in a saucepan and leave overnight. Add the lemon juice and proceed as described for the plum or nectarine jam (see above recipe). Spoon into clean, sterilised jars.

Makes about 3-4 honey jars.

Mock fig jam

You need a few fig leaves for this delicious recipe sent in by Mrs Nill Mey of Parkdene, Boksburg. This jam smells and tastes just like real fig jam, but is made with green tomatoes.

- 1 kg green tomatoes, skinned and cut into small, neat pieces
- 1 whole piece fresh ginger
- 8-10 fig leaves
- sugar
- 15 ml (1 T) lemon juice (optional)

Heat the tomatoes in a saucepan along with the ginger and fig leaves. Cook slowly until the tomatoes are soft. Add a little water if necessary. Remove the fig leaves.

Weigh the tomato pulp and add the same quantity sugar. (Add the lemon juice if preferred.) Return to the heat. Stir continuously to dissolve the sugar before the mixture comes to the boil. Boil slowly until the jam is fairly thick and no longer watery. (Drop a little jam on a saucer and cool – if it is no longer runny, the jam is ready.) Spoon into clean, sterilised jars.

Makes about 500 ml jam.

Orange marmalade

What could be nicer than orange marmalade on hot toast for breakfast? Mrs Alba van der Walt of Leeudoringstad has been making this marmalade for years, using a very different method to the traditional one for making jam.

- 8 medium oranges, seeded and cut into small pieces (reserve the skins)
- 16 x 250 ml (16 c) sugar
- 5 litres (20 x 250 ml) water

Place the oranges, along with the skins, in a food processor and process.

Place the orange pulp, sugar and water in a large saucepan. Stir well until the sugar has dissolved. Bring to the boil and cook for about 8 hours or until the jam is no longer runny when a little is spooned onto a saucer and has cooled.

Spoon into clean, sterilised jars and seal while hot.

Makes 2,5 litres marmalade.

Orange marmalade

Apple and naartjie jam

Mrs Josie Olivier of Heuwelsig, Bloemfontein makes a deliciously unusual jam with apples and naartjies. She writes she sometimes uses the jam as a filling for tartlets.

- 4 medium green apples, peeled and grated (reserve the skins and cores)
- 2 large naartjies (peeled and pips removed and reserved), cut into small pieces
- juice of 1 large lemon (reserve skin and pips)
- 2,5 litres (10 x 250 ml) water
- 7 x 250 ml (7 c) sugar

Place the grated apples, naartjie pieces and lemon juice in a large saucepan, preferably stainless steel. Add the water.

Tie up all the skins and pips in a piece of cheesecloth and add to the saucepan. Bring to the boil and boil for 30

Apple and naartjie jam

minutes. Cool completely. (For the best results, leave the cheesecloth bag in the mixture overnight.)

Remove the cheesecloth bag from the saucepan. Press out all the liquid and add to the fruit mixture. Discard the cheesecloth bag and its contents.

Add the sugar to the fruit mixture and heat. Stir continuously until all the sugar has dissolved and before the mixture comes to the boil. (Remove the sugar crystals that form on the sides of the saucepan with a wet brush or cover the saucepan with a lid for about 3 minutes to allow the crystals to dissolve.) Bring the mixture to the boil and boil until it is thick and no longer watery. (Spoon a little of the jam into a saucer and cool – if it is no longer runny, the jam is ready.) Spoon into clean, sterilised jars.

Makes about 1,5 litres jam.

Hunter's pâté

The members of the Vredendal women's agricultural organisation always serve this pâté at their functions.

- 12,5 ml (2½ t) butter
- 2 onions, grated
- 100 g bacon, chopped
- 500 g pork sausages
- hot water
- 4 medium potatoes, peeled, boiled and mashed
- 1 apple, grated
- 12,5 ml (2½ t) finely chopped red and green pepper
- 25 ml (5 t) finely chopped parsley
- 15 ml (1 T) hot chutney
- 3 ml (generous ½ t) dried thyme
- 3 ml (generous ½ t) chicken stock cube, crumbled
- pinch celery salt
- freshly ground black pepper
- 1 egg, whisked
- 125 ml (½ c) red wine
- 25 ml (5 t) sherry or sweet hanepoot wine
- few bay leaves or fresh sprig of herbs

Preheat the oven to 150 °C (300 °F). Grease an ovenproof dish or a small 21 x 11 x 7-cm loaf tin with butter or margarine, or spray with nonstick spray.

Heat the butter in a pan and sauté the onions and bacon until tender and cooked.

Place the pork sausages in very hot water and prick the casings with a fork to release the fat. Leave in the water for 5 minutes.

Remove the meat from the casings and combine it with the remaining ingredients.

Place the bay leaves or fresh sprig of herbs in a greased dish or tin and spoon the mixture on top. Cover with aluminium foil and bake for about 1 hour.

Cool and serve the pâté with bread.
Serves 6-8.

Hummus

Hummus is one of the delicacies you'll find at the Barnyard farmstall in Tokai near Cape Town. It's a spread made with chickpeas and it goes beautifully with their spinach muffins or whole-wheat seed bread (see recipes, pp. 50 and 13).

- 250 ml (1 c) chickpeas, soaked in water overnight
- 2 cloves garlic, crushed
- juice of 1 lemon
- salt and freshly ground black pepper
- olive oil for pouring on top
- paprika for sprinkling on top

Pour off the soaking water and boil the chickpeas in fresh water until soft. Drain, but reserve about 125 ml (½ c) of the water.

Mash the chickpeas with 125 ml drained water. Add the garlic, lemon juice, salt and pepper and mix to form a spread. Spoon into a dish and pour over a little olive oil. Sprinkle with paprika.

Makes about 500 ml (2 c).

Chicken liver pâté

You can make a meal of bread and pâté at the Barnyard farmstall in Tokai near Cape Town.

- 1 tub (250 g) chicken livers, cleaned
- salt and freshly ground black pepper
- 225 g butter (at room temperature)
- 30 ml (2 T) brandy
- 15 ml (1 T) mustard powder
- 2 ml (½ t) thyme
- 2 cloves garlic, crushed

Season the chicken livers to taste with salt and pepper. Melt 25 g of the butter and fry the chicken livers over medium heat until brown on the outside but still slightly pink inside. Remove from the pan and place in the food processor.

Melt 150 g of the butter and add to the chicken livers. Add the brandy to the pan juices in the pan, mixing well. Add the mixture to the chicken livers in the food processor. Add the seasoning and garlic.

Process until smooth and season with salt and pepper if necessary. Spoon into a dish, melt the remaining butter and pour on top. Chill until the butter has set.

Serve with whole-wheat bread.
Makes about 250 g.

Winning rusks

What a treat to be served coffee and rusks in bed over a weekend. And if you run a busy household you probably won't be able to rustle up a quicker breakfast. A tin filled with rusks is also a must if you have permanently hungry kids in the house. Rusks are good for the whole family, especially if made with wholesome ingredients such as bran and seeds. This chapter contains every possible kind of rusk recipe – buttermilk rusks, whole-wheat rusks, rusks for the busy housewife . . . We've even included a recipe for old-fashioned mosbolletjies (must buns).

Egg-free rusks

Andrea Potgieter of Sasolburg was given this recipe by a friend. The rusks contain no eggs and are deliciously coarse because of all the bran. Andrea says she often baked these rusks for the nursing staff who cared for her baby while in the intensive care unit at the Unie Hospital in Alberton. They now all bake it regularly.

- 1 kg self-raising flour
- pinch salt
- 8 x 250 ml (8 c) digestive bran
- 250 ml (1 c) sugar
- 250 ml (1 c) raisins
- 500 g margarine, melted
- 1 litre (4 x 250 ml) milk

Preheat the oven to 180 °C (350 °F). Spray a 28 x 38-cm deep, black oven pan with nonstick spray or grease well with butter or margarine.

Combine the self-raising flour, salt and bran. Add the sugar and raisins and mix. Add the melted margarine to the dry ingredients, alternating with the milk. Mix well. Turn the mixture into the prepared oven pan, spreading evenly.

Bake for 30 minutes or until done and a testing skewer comes out clean when inserted into the centre of the rusk mixture. Cool slightly before turning out onto a wire rack to cool completely.

Break into pieces, place on a baking sheet and dry out at 100 °C (200 °F). Store in an airtight container.

Makes about 47 rusks.

Rich buttermilk rusks

Elna de Klerk of Bellville experimented with her usual recipe for buttermilk rusks, resulting in these rich, flavoursome rusks.

- 1 kg self-raising flour
- 10 ml (2 t) baking powder
- 5 ml (1 t) mixed spice
- 5 ml (1 t) salt
- 250 ml (1 c) sugar
- 375 ml (1 ½ c) coconut
- 50 ml (⅕ c) sesame seeds
- 250 g butter, grated
- 2 extra-large eggs
- 1 container (250 ml) sour cream
- 250 ml (1 c) buttermilk or milk
- 5 ml (1 t) lemon essence

Preheat the oven to 180 °C (350 °F). Spray a 28 x 38-cm deep, black oven pan with nonstick spray or grease well with butter or margarine.

Combine all the dry ingredients. Rub in the butter with your fingertips until the mixture resembles breadcrumbs. Whisk the eggs, sour cream, buttermilk and lemon essence together and add to the dry ingredients. Mix until a soft, manageable dough is formed. Roll into balls and pack into the prepared pan or, if preferred, turn the mixture into the pan.

Bake for 50 minutes or until done and a testing skewer comes out clean when inserted into the centre of the rusk mixture. Cool slightly before turning out onto a wire rack to cool completely. Break into pieces and arrange on a baking sheet. Dry out at 100 °C (200 °F). Store in an airtight container.

Makes about 34 rusks.

Front, from left to right: Easy microwaved health rusks (p. 106), Rich buttermilk rusks, Egg-free rusks and Tannie Neethling's rusks (p. 36, in oven pan)

Tannie Neethling's rusks

Mrs I.A. du Plessis of Parow was given this recipe by her neighbour, Tannie Neethling. Mrs Du Plessis says no one can beat her neighbour when it comes to making rusks.

- 4 x 500-g packets self-raising flour
- 10 ml (2 t) aniseed
- 10 ml (2 t) salt
- 500 ml (2 c) sugar
- 500 g margarine, melted
- 750 ml-1 litre (3-4 c) milk
- 4 eggs, whisked

Preheat the oven to 180 °C (350 °F). Spray a 40 x 27-cm deep, black oven pan with nonstick spray or grease well with butter or margarine.

Combine the self-raising flour, aniseed, salt and sugar in a large mixing bowl. Beat the margarine, milk and eggs and add to the dry ingredients. Mix well to form a stiff dough. Roll into balls and arrange in the prepared pan.

Bake for 45 minutes or until done. The rusks are done when a testing skewer comes out clean when inserted into the centre of the rusk mixture. Cool slightly before turning out onto a wire rack to cool completely. Break into pieces, place on a baking sheet and dry out at 100 °C (200 °F).

Switch on the oven grill and brown the rusks lightly if preferred, taking care not to overdo it. Store in an airtight container.

Makes about 50 rusks.

Winning rusks

Every home should have a constant supply of these absolutely delicious rusks, writes Mrs Rika Neethling of Secunda. The pecan nuts impart a rich flavour to the rusks.

- 1,25 kg self-raising flour
- 5 ml (1 t) salt
- 15 ml (1 T) baking powder
- 375 ml (1½ c) sugar
- 300 g butter or margarine
- 5 x 250 ml (5 c) All Bran Flakes
- 1 packet (100 g) pecan nuts, coarsely chopped
- 2 extra-large eggs
- 375 ml (1½ c) buttermilk

Preheat the oven to 180 °C (350 °F). Grease a large 37 x 13 x 10-cm loaf tin well with butter or margarine, or spray with nonstick spray.

Sift the self-raising flour, salt and baking powder together. Add the sugar and mix. Rub in the butter with your fingertips until the mixture resembles breadcrumbs. Add the All Bran Flakes and pecan nuts and mix.

Beat the eggs and buttermilk together and add to the flour mixture. Mix well. Turn into the prepared loaf tin, spreading evenly. Bake for about 50 minutes or until the rusks are pale brown on top and baked through, and a testing skewer comes out clean when inserted into the centre of the rusk mixture. Turn out onto a wire rack and cool slightly. Cut into fingers and dry out at 100 °C (200 °F). Store in airtight containers.

Makes about 60 rusks.

Yummy rusks

Her two children and their university pals agree: these are the best rusks in the world, writes Mrs Johanna Jacoby of Kimberley.

- 750 g margarine
- 4 x 250 ml (4 c) sugar
- 1 litre (4 x 250 ml) boiling water
- 6 x 500-g packets self-raising flour
- 50 ml (⅕ c) baking powder
- 15 ml (1 T) bicarbonate of soda
- 15 ml (1 T) cream of tartar
- 5 ml (1 t) salt
- 150 g All Bran Flakes
- 150 g Corn Flakes
- 830 ml (3⅓ c) bran
- 300 ml (1⅕ c) coconut
- 5 extra-large eggs, whisked

Preheat the oven to 180 °C (350 °F). Spray two 38 x 28-cm black oven pans with nonstick spray or grease well with butter or margarine.

Heat the margarine, sugar and boiling water in a large saucepan until the sugar has dissolved and the margarine melted. Set aside.

Sift the self-raising flour, baking powder, bicarbonate of soda, cream of tartar and salt together in a large mixing bowl. Add the breakfast cereals, bran and coconut and mix well.

Add the margarine mixture to the dry ingredients, alternating with the eggs. Mix well with a wooden spoon. Roll into balls and arrange in the prepared oven pans.

Bake for 60-80 minutes or until done and a testing skewer comes out clean when inserted into the centre of the rusk mixture. Cool slightly before turning out onto a wire rack to cool completely. Break into pieces and dry out at 100 °C (200 °F). Store in airtight containers.

Makes about 128 rusks.

Easy rusks

Mrs A. Conradie of Worcester says she has to bake a batch of these rusks every week because they disappear so quickly.

- 1 litre (4 x 250 ml) boiling water
- 500 g margarine, cut into pieces
- 500 ml (2 c) sugar
- 3 extra-large eggs, whisked
- 4 x 500-g packets self-raising flour
- 15 ml (1 T) baking powder
- 5 ml (1 t) salt

Preheat the oven to 180 °C (350 °F). Spray a 37 x 27-cm black oven pan with nonstick spray or grease well with butter or margarine.

Pour the boiling water over the margarine and stir until melted. Add the sugar, stirring until dissolved. Add the eggs and mix.

In a large mixing bowl, sift together the self-raising flour, baking powder and salt. Add the margarine mixture and mix. Knead until well blended. Add more self-raising flour if the dough sticks to your hands. Turn into the prepared oven pan. Cover with greased plastic wrap and leave to rise for 30 minutes in the warming drawer or in a warm place until the dough has doubled in volume. Remove the plastic wrap and bake for 60 minutes or until a testing skewer comes out clean when inserted into the centre of the rusks. Turn out onto a wire rack and cool. Cut into pieces and place on a baking sheet. Dry out overnight at 100 °C (200 °F). Store in airtight containers.

Makes about 75 rusks.

Whole-wheat buttermilk rusks

Margaret le Roux of Oudtshoorn writes these fibre-packed, egg-free rusks are quick and easy to make. She was given the recipe years ago by a friend.

- 9 x 250 ml (9 c) whole-wheat flour
- 4 x 250 ml (4 c) cake flour
- 45 ml (3 T) custard powder
- 25 ml (5 t) bicarbonate of soda
- 15 ml (1 T) cream of tartar
- 20 ml (4 t) salt
- 500 ml (2 c) sugar
- 1,5 litres (6 x 250 ml) buttermilk
- 500 ml (2 c) oil
- 60 ml (¼ c) white grape vinegar

Preheat the oven to 180 °C (350 °F). Spray two large 34 x 11 x 7-cm loaf tins with nonstick spray or grease well with butter or margarine. Sprinkle a little whole-wheat flour on the base and along the sides of the tins.

Sift the whole-wheat flour, cake flour, custard powder, bicarbonate of soda, cream of tartar and salt together in a large mixing bowl. Add the bran left behind in the sieve. Add the sugar to the flour mixture and mix well.

Blend the buttermilk, oil and grape vinegar and add to the dry ingredients. Mix well with a wooden spoon. Turn into the prepared tins, spreading evenly. Bake for 1 hour or until baked through and pale brown on top, and a testing skewer comes out clean when inserted into the centre of the rusk mixture. Cool slightly before turning out onto wire racks to cool. Cut into pieces and dry out at 100 °C (200 °F). Store in airtight containers.

Makes 110 rusks.

Busy housewife's rusks

Bessie Impey of Wierda Park uses this recipe to bake white and whole-wheat rusks in an oven pan. Her recipe did not call for any sugar, but we added a cupful. Without the sugar the rusks taste just as good.

- 15 ml (1 T) vinegar
- 350-400 ml (1⅖-1⅗ c) milk
- 1 extra-large egg, whisked
- 300 g margarine, melted
- 1 kg self-raising flour
- 250 ml (1 c) sugar (optional)
- 5 ml (1 t) salt

Preheat the oven to 180 °C (350 °F). Spray a 37 x 27-cm black oven pan with nonstick spray or grease well with butter or margarine.

Mix the vinegar, milk and egg together and add to the melted margarine.

Combine the dry ingredients and add the margarine mixture to form a soft dough. Turn into the prepared pan. Spread evenly and mark off fingers.

Bake for about 40 minutes or until a testing skewer comes out clean when inserted into the centre of the rusks. Cool for about 10 minutes in the pan, turn out and cool a little longer before breaking into fingers. Arrange on baking sheets. Dry out at 100 °C (200 °F). Store in airtight containers.

Makes about 25 rusks.

Variation

- **To make whole-wheat rusks:** Substitute 750 ml (3 c) cake flour, 4 x 250 ml (4 c) whole-wheat flour and 45 ml (3 T) baking powder for the self-raising flour. Proceed as described in the basic recipe. Makes about 25 rusks.

Egg-free bran rusks

Whenever she makes these delicious rusks she intends sending us the recipe because it's so easy and economical, writes Rina Viljoen of Kakamas. The ingredients may be varied by, for instance, adding seeds or raisins or using whole-wheat flour instead of bran. This is also an egg-free recipe.

- 450 g margarine
- 500 ml (2 c) boiling water
- 250 ml (1 c) sugar
- 4 x 250 ml (4 c) brown bread flour
- 5 x 250 ml (5 c) bran
- 250 ml (1 c) coconut
- 30 ml (2 T) baking powder
- 5 ml (1 t) salt

Preheat the oven to 180 °C (350 °F). Spray a 38 x 28-cm black oven pan with nonstick spray or grease well with butter or margarine.

Melt the margarine in 100 ml (⅖ c) of the boiling water. Add the remaining boiling water to the sugar, stirring well until the sugar has dissolved. Add to the margarine mixture, mixing well.

Combine the dry ingredients and add the margarine mixture. Mix well with a wooden spoon. Turn into the prepared oven pan and cut into squares.

Bake for 30 minutes. Reduce heat to 160 °C (325 °F) and bake another 30 minutes or until done and a testing skewer comes out clean when inserted into the centre of the rusk mixture. Cool slightly and break into squares. Dry out at 100 °C (200 °F).

Store in airtight containers.

Makes about 36 rusks.

From bottom left, clockwise: Whole-wheat buttermilk rusks (p. 37), Egg-free bran rusks and Yummy rusks (p. 36)

Bran rusks

This reader, who unfortunately forgot to send us her name, writes she first tasted these rusks in America. Apparently the Americans love having a snack at about nine on a cold winter's evening. These rusks, fresh from the oven and buttered while still hot, are a great favourite.

- 1 kg self-raising flour
- 5 ml (1 t) salt
- 500 ml (2 c) sugar
- 7 x 250 ml (7 c) bran
- 500 g butter or margarine
- 650 ml (2⅗ c) milk

Preheat the oven to 180 °C (350 °F). Spray a large 37 x 13 x 7-cm loaf tin with nonstick spray or grease well with butter or margarine.

Sift the self-raising flour and salt together. Add the sugar and bran and mix well. Rub in the butter or margarine with your fingertips until evenly blended and the mixture resembles breadcrumbs. Add the milk and mix well. Turn into the prepared tin, spreading evenly.

Bake for about 1 hour or until pale brown and a testing skewer comes out clean when inserted into the centre of the rusks. Turn out onto a wire rack and cool slightly. Cut into fingers and arrange on a baking sheet. Dry out at 100 °C (200 °F) and store in an airtight container.

Makes about 60 rusks.

Sunflower seed rusks

Mrs H. Diedericks of Bethlehem writes everyone in her family has these rusks for breakfast. The rusks contain no eggs.

- 500 g margarine
- 750 ml (3 c) plain yoghurt
- 1 kg self-raising flour
- 10 ml (2 t) baking powder
- 10 ml (2 t) salt
- 5 x 250 ml (5 c) bran
- 625 ml (2½ c) All Bran Flakes
- 625 ml (2½ c) sunflower seeds
- 250 ml (1 c) brown sugar

Preheat the oven to 180 °C (350 °F). Spray a 37 x 27 x 5-cm black oven pan with nonstick spray or grease well with butter or margarine.

Melt the margarine and add the yoghurt. Set aside.

Sift the self-raising flour, baking powder and salt together in a large mixing bowl. Add the remaining dry ingredients and mix lightly. Add the margarine and

yoghurt mixture and mix until well blended. Turn into the prepared oven pan and bake for 40 minutes or until a testing skewer comes out clean when inserted into the centre of the rusks. Cool the rusks slightly in the pan before turning out onto a wire rack. Cool completely and cut into pieces. Place on a baking sheet and dry out at 100 °C (200 °F). Store in airtight containers.

Makes about 60 rusks.

Super health rusks

These rusks are filling and packed with fibre, writes Mrs D. Retief of Hanover.

- 4 x 250 ml (4 c) self-raising flour
- 25 ml (5 t) baking powder
- 10 ml (2 t) salt
- 500 ml (2 c) whole-wheat flour
- 500 ml (2 c) Weet-Bix, crushed
- 250 ml (1 c) muesli
- 200 ml (⅘ c) sunflower seeds
- 50 ml (⅕ c) bran
- 500 g butter
- 500 ml (2 c) buttermilk or plain yoghurt
- 450 ml (1⅘ c) sugar
- 50 ml (⅕ c) honey
- 10 ml (2 t) brown vinegar
- 2 large eggs

Preheat the oven to 200 °C (400 °F). Spray two 29 x 12 x 7-cm loaf tins with nonstick spray or grease well with butter or margarine.

Sift together the self-raising flour, baking powder and salt. Add the whole-wheat flour, Weet-Bix, muesli, sunflower seeds and bran. Grate in the butter and rub until well blended.

Whisk together the buttermilk, sugar, honey, vinegar and eggs. Add to the flour mixture and turn into the tins, spreading the mixture evenly. Bake for about 40-60 minutes or until a testing skewer comes out clean when inserted into the centre of the rusks. Turn out, cool slightly and cut into fingers. Arrange the rusks on baking sheets and dry out at 100 °C (200 °F) until completely dry.

Store in airtight containers.

Makes about 36 large rusks.

Mosbolletjies (must buns) and rusks

Although these mosbolletjies are not made with traditional raisin yeast they taste just like the real thing. We sampled these delicacies at the meat festival in Calvinia one year. Ounooi de Klerk, a first-rate baker in the district, gave us her prized recipe.

- 125 g butter or margarine
- 500 ml (2 c) sugar
- 500 ml (2 c) boiled milk
- 500 ml (2 c) boiling water
- 2 eggs, whisked
- 1 packet (10 g) dry yeast (not instant yeast), dissolved in 125 ml (½ c) lukewarm water
- 30 ml (2 T) honey
- 500 ml (2 c) cake flour
- 1,5 kg cake flour or brown bread flour
- 10 ml (2 t) salt
- 30 ml (2 T) aniseed, cinnamon or shredded naartjie peel
- 5 ml (1 t) sugar
- 15 ml (1 T) milk

Preheat the oven to 180 °C (350 °F). Grease three 29 x 12 x 7-cm loaf tins with butter or margarine or spray with nonstick spray.

Place the butter and sugar in a mixing bowl and pour over the milk and boiling water. Stir until melted and cool to room temperature.

Add the eggs, dissolved dried yeast and honey, and mix. Add the 500 ml (2 c) cake flour and mix well. Cover and leave in a warm place to rise until air bubbles form on top.

Add the 1,5 kg cake flour, salt and aniseed to the yeast mixture, mix and knead for about 15-20 minutes or until the dough is smooth and elastic. (Add a little cakeflour if necessary.) Cover with greased plastic wrap and leave to rise until double in bulk.

Knock back the dough, grease your hands with butter and break off small balls of dough. Arrange the balls of dough in the prepared tins, tilting the tins slightly. Brush the dough balls with melted butter on top and in between. Cover and leave to rise in a warm place until the dough fills the tins.

Bake for 40-60 minutes or until done. Dissolve the sugar in the milk and brush the mosbolletjies with the mixture. Bake for another 5 minutes. Turn out onto a wire rack to cool slightly.

Break into balls and serve with butter. Alternatively, cut the balls into smaller pieces, if preferred, and dry out at 100 °C (200 °F).

Makes 3 tins of mosbolletjies.

Skuinskoek

Skuinskoek is usually made of leftover mosbolletjie dough which is deep-fried.

Prepare the dough as described in the mosbolletjie recipe and leave to rise until double in volume. Knock back and break into pieces. Roll into long, thin rolls about 3 cm thick. Cut the rolls of dough into 3-cm long pieces and leave to rise slightly.

Heat sufficient oil in a deep saucepan and fry the skuinskoek until golden brown and done inside. Drain on paper towelling.

Marvellous muffins

It takes very little time and effort to bake a delicious batch of muffins. Serve them for breakfast or pack them into the kids' lunch box or picnic basket. Muffins are a wonderful tea-time treat, excellent with a glass of wine, and the perfect in-between snack. In fact, muffins can be served any time of day, no matter what the occasion.

Bulk muffins

This recipe, sent in by Mrs Marie Carratu of Suider-Paarl, appeared in *Winning Recipes 2*, but we're repeating it due to popular demand. The muffins have a soft texture and are best served with just a bit of butter.

Over the years the recipe has been adapted and is now made with less sugar and fat. The batter lasts for about a month in the fridge. Bake as many muffins as you need (the recipe makes about 60, depending on the size of the tins) and add whatever takes your fancy.

- 4 x 250 ml (4 c) bran
- 500 ml (2 c) oats
- 625 ml (2½ c) boiling water
- 125 ml (½ c) oil
- 250 ml (1 c) brown sugar
- 4 eggs, whisked
- 1 litre (4 x 250 ml) buttermilk
- 25 ml (5 t) bicarbonate of soda
- 625 ml (2½ c) cake flour
- 625 ml (2½ c) whole-wheat flour
- 10 ml (2 t) salt
- additions: chopped mixed dried fruit, chopped nuts, coarsely chopped apple or banana or grated carrot to taste

Combine the bran, oats and boiling water. Add the oil and cool slightly. Add the sugar, eggs and 750 ml (3 c) of the buttermilk and mix. Blend the remaining 250 ml (1 c) buttermilk and bicarbonate of soda and add. Add the dry ingredients and mix.

Transfer the mixture to clean jars, close tightly and store in the fridge until needed.

Preheat the oven to 220 °C (425 °F). Spray a muffin tin with 12 hollows with nonstick spray or grease well with butter or margarine.

Add any of the additions: Use about 250 ml (1 c)

From bottom left, clockwise: Pizza muffins (p. 47), Apple crumble muffins (p. 44), Chocolate and banana muffins (p. 44) and Health muffins

per 500 ml (2 c) batter and fill the muffin tin hollows two-thirds of the way. Bake for about 20 minutes or until done. Cool slightly in the tin before turning out onto a wire rack to cool completely.

Makes about 60 muffins.

Health muffins

Val Burns, who lives near Hazyview, sent us a selection of muffin recipes. This is a healthy alternative.

- 250 ml (1 c) self-raising flour
- 250 ml (1 c) coconut
- 125 ml (½ c) oats
- 125 ml (½ c) brown sugar
- 100 ml (⅖ c) sesame seeds
- 100 ml (⅖ c) whole-wheat flour
- 100 ml (⅖ c) raisins
- 100 ml (⅖ c) melted butter
- 15 ml (1 T) honey
- 1 extra-large egg, whisked
- 150 ml (⅗ c) milk
- 1 slab (100 g) white chocolate (optional)

Preheat the oven to 180 °C (350 °F). Spray two muffin tins with 12 hollows each with nonstick spray or grease well with butter or margarine.

Combine all the dry ingredients and raisins in a large mixing bowl.

Blend the butter and honey and add to the dry ingredients, mixing lightly. Blend the egg and milk and add to the flour mixture. Mix lightly, taking care not to overmix. Fill the muffin tin hollows three-quarters of the way with the batter and bake for 20 minutes or until done. The muffins are done when a testing skewer comes out clean when inserted into the centre of the muffins. Cool in the tin for a few minutes before turning out onto a wire rack to cool completely.

Melt chocolate and drizzle over muffins if preferred.

Makes 15 muffins.

Chocolate and banana muffins

Chocolate-flavoured muffins. Another recipe from Val Burns.

- 75 g creamed cottage cheese
- 30 ml (2 T) caster sugar
- 3 large bananas, peeled and mashed
- 180 ml (¾ c) sugar
- 1 extra-large egg, whisked
- 80 ml (⅓ c) melted butter
- 375 ml (1½ c) cake flour
- 45 ml (3 T) cocoa
- 5 ml (1 t) baking powder
- 5 ml (1 t) bicarbonate of soda
- pinch salt
- icing sugar for dusting

Preheat the oven to 190 °C (375 °F). Spray a muffin tin with 12 hollows with nonstick spray or grease well with butter or margarine.

Beat the creamed cottage cheese and caster sugar together until well blended. Set aside.

Mix the mashed banana, sugar, egg and melted butter. Set aside.

Sift together the cake flour, cocoa, baking powder, bicarbonate of soda and salt in a large mixing bowl. Add the banana mixture and mix lightly until just blended. Fill the muffin tin hollows halfway with the batter and spoon a teaspoonful of the cottage cheese mixture on top. Spoon more of the muffin batter on top, filling the muffin tin hollows three-quarters of the way. Bake for 10-12 minutes or until the muffins are done and a testing skewer comes out clean when inserted into the centre of the muffins. Cool in the tin for a few minutes before turning out onto a wire rack to cool completely.

Dust with icing sugar if preferred.

Makes 12 muffins.

Apple crumble muffins

Another mouthwatering recipe sent in by Val Burns. Delicious served with butter or whipped cream.

TOPPING
- 100 g walnuts, chopped
- 60 ml (¼ c) cake flour
- 15 ml (1 T) sugar
- 1 ml (¼ t) cinnamon
- 1 ml (¼ t) cloves
- 30 ml (2 T) butter

BATTER
- 375 ml (1½ c) cake flour
- 10 ml (2 t) baking powder
- 2 ml (½ t) bicarbonate of soda
- 7 ml (1½ t) mixed spice
- 2 ml (½ t) salt
- 125 ml (½ c) sugar
- 2 extra-large eggs, whisked
- 250 ml (1 c) buttermilk
- 250 ml (1 c) grated cooking apple
  (2 small apples, peeled)

Preheat the oven to 180 °C (350 °F). Spray a muffin tin with 12 hollows with nonstick spray or grease well with butter or margarine.

■ TOPPING: Mix the walnuts and dry ingredients for the topping and rub in the butter with your fingertips until well blended. Set aside.

■ BATTER: In a large mixing bowl, sift together the cake flour, baking powder, bicarbonate of soda, mixed spice and salt. Add the sugar and mix.

Mix the eggs and buttermilk and add the grated apple. Add to the dry ingredients, mixing lightly until just blended. Fill the muffin tin hollows three-quarters of the way with the batter. Make a slight hollow in the centre of each muffin and fill with a teaspoonful of the topping.

Bake for 20 minutes or until a testing skewer comes out clean when inserted into the centre of the muffins. Cool slightly in the tin before turning out onto a wire rack to cool completely.

Serve with butter or whipped cream.

Makes 12 muffins.

Carrot and poppy seed muffins

Honey adds sweetness to these muffins, while whole-wheat flour, mealie meal and poppy seeds provide the fibre, writes Elna Mattheus of Pretoria. The muffins contain no milk – apple juice is used instead.

- 250 ml (1 c) cake flour
- 180 ml (¾ c) whole-wheat flour
- 250 ml (1 c) mealie meal
- 15 ml (1 T) baking powder
- 3 ml (generous ½ t) bicarbonate of soda
- 60 ml (¼ c) poppy seeds
- 250 ml (1 c) apple juice
- 2 extra-large eggs
- 125 ml (½ c) honey
- 60 ml (¼ c) oil
- 250 ml (1 c) grated carrots

Preheat the oven to 190 °C (375 °F). Spray a muffin tin with 12 hollows, with nonstick spray or grease well with butter or margarine.

Sift together the cake flour, whole-wheat flour, mealie meal, baking powder and bicarbonate of soda.

Add the bran left behind in the sieve and the poppy seeds and mix lightly.

Whisk together the apple juice, eggs, honey and oil. Add to the dry ingredients. Add the carrots and fold in lightly until just blended. Fill the muffin tin hollows three-quarters of the way and bake for 20-25 minutes or until a testing skewer comes out clean when inserted into the centre of the muffins.

Serve with butter, cheese and honey.

Makes 12-15 large muffins.

Carrot and poppy seed muffins

Pizza muffins

These muffins have a real pizza flavour. The recipe was sent in by Val Burns.

- 1 large tomato, skinned and finely chopped
- 2 ml (½ t) sugar
- 500 ml (2 c) cake flour
- 5 ml (1 t) origanum
- 2 ml (½ t) salt
- 1 ml (¼ t) black pepper
- 10 ml (2 t) baking powder
- 30 ml (2 T) olive oil
- 1 large clove garlic, crushed
- 12 black olives, stoned and halved
- 1 extra-large egg, whisked
- 180 ml (¾ c) water
- 125 ml (½ c) grated Cheddar cheese
- little cayenne pepper

Preheat the oven to 200 °C (400 °F). Spray a muffin tin with 12 hollows with nonstick spray or grease well with butter or margarine.

Mix the tomato and sugar and set aside.

Sift together the dry ingredients and add the olive oil, garlic and olives. Mix. Mix the egg and water and add. Mix lightly until just blended and fill the muffin tin hollows three-quarters of the way with the batter.

Make a hollow in the centre of each muffin and fill with a teaspoonful of the tomato mixture. Sprinkle with a little cheese and a little cayenne pepper.

Bake for 15-20 minutes or until a testing skewer comes out clean when inserted into the centre of the muffins. Serve hot.

Makes 10 muffins.

Quick spiced muffins

Bake these muffins instead of hot cross buns. Prepare them a day or two in advance and store in an airtight container.

- 4 x 250 ml (4 c) cake flour
- 25 ml (5 t) baking powder
- 2 ml (½ t) salt
- 15 ml (1 T) mixed spice
- 5 ml (1 t) ground cinnamon
- 200 g margarine
- 200 ml (⅘ c) soft brown sugar
- 500 ml (2 c) dried fruitcake mix
- 1 egg
- 375 ml (1½ c) milk

Gemsbok biltong and blue cheese muffins

Preheat the oven to 190 °C (375 °F). Grease the hollows of two muffin tins with butter or margarine, or spray with nonstick spray.

Sift the dry ingredients together and rub in the margarine with your fingertips until the mixture resembles breadcrumbs.

Add the brown sugar and dried fruitcake mix. Whisk the egg and milk together and add to the mixture. Mix lightly until just blended – the mixture must still be slightly lumpy.

Fill the muffin tin hollows two-thirds of the way with the batter and bake for 20-25 minutes or until a testing skewer comes out clean when inserted into the centre of the muffins.

Cool slightly in the tins before turning out onto a wire rack to cool completely.

Serve with margarine.

Makes about 24-30 muffins.

Gemsbok biltong and blue cheese muffins

For a taste of the Kalahari, try these muffins from Le Must, Niel Stemmet's restaurant in Upington.

- 5 extra-large eggs
- 500 ml (2 c) buttermilk
- 180 ml (¾ c) olive oil
- 500 g self-raising flour
- 750 ml (3 c) cake flour
- 10 ml (2 t) bicarbonate of soda
- 10 ml (2 t) baking powder
- 5 ml (1 t) salt
- 2 ml (½ t) paprika
- 250 ml (1 c) currants, soaked in port and water
- 500 ml (2 c) gemsbok biltong, chopped and soaked in dry sherry
- 500 ml (2 c) grated blue cheese
- few sprigs finely chopped rosemary
- melted butter

Preheat the oven to 200 °C (400 °F). Spray a few muffin tins with nonstick spray or grease well with butter or margarine.

In a large mixing bowl, beat together the eggs, buttermilk and olive oil with a wooden spoon. Add the remaining ingredients, mixing well.

Fill the hollows of the muffin tins three-quarters of the way and bake for about 20 minutes or until a testing skewer comes out clean when inserted into the centre of the muffins. Remove from the oven and glaze the crusts with a little melted butter.

Serve hot or cold with Marmite butter and real coffee.

Makes 45 medium muffins.

Tomato and basil muffins

Val Moodley of Mayfair makes these delicious muffins flavoured with tomatoes and basil.

- 500 ml (2 c) cake flour
- 10 ml (2 t) baking powder
- 5 ml (1 t) salt
- 15 ml (1 T) sugar
- 5 ml (1 t) mustard powder
- 2 extra-large eggs
- 250 ml (1 c) milk
- 125 g butter, melted
- 20 ml (4 t) tomato paste
- 1 ripe tomato, skinned and finely chopped
- 25 ml (5 t) freshly chopped basil
- 15 ml (1 T) finely chopped chives

Preheat the oven to 180 °C (350 °F). Spray a muffin tin with 12 hollows with nonstick spray or grease well with butter or margarine.

In a large mixing bowl, sift together the cake flour, baking powder, salt, sugar and mustard powder.

Whisk together the eggs, milk and butter. Add the tomato paste and tomato, mixing well. Add the basil and chives. Add to the dry ingredients, folding in lightly until just blended.

Fill the prepared muffin tins three-quarters of the way with the mixture. Bake for 10-15 minutes or until a testing skewer comes out clean when inserted into the centre of the muffins.

Serve lukewarm with butter.

Makes 11-12 large muffins.

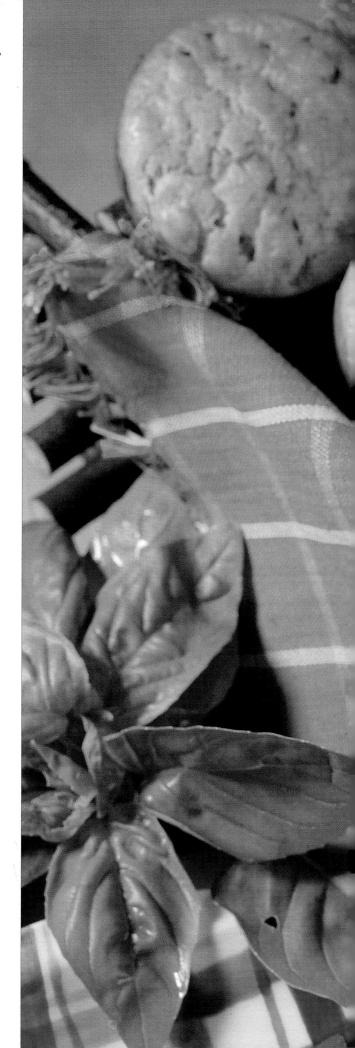

Tomato and basil muffins

Spinach muffins

One of our regular readers wrote in asking for a recipe for spinach muffins with feta cheese. Although this recipe, sent in by Tembisa Nodada of Port Elizabeth, calls for Cheddar cheese, the muffins are just as good if made with feta cheese.

- 375 ml (1½ c) cake flour
- 10 ml (2 t) baking powder
- 2 ml (½ t) salt
- pinch nutmeg or cayenne pepper
- 250 ml (1 c) cooked spinach, chopped
- 250 ml (1 c) feta cheese, crumbled
- 100 ml (⅖ c) milk
- 100 ml (⅖ c) oil
- 1 egg

Preheat the oven to 190 °C (375 °F). Spray a muffin tin with 12 hollows with nonstick spray or grease well with butter or margarine.

Sift the dry ingredients together in a mixing bowl. Add the spinach and cheese, mixing lightly.

Whisk the milk, oil and egg together and add to the dry ingredients. Mix until just blended but still lumpy. Turn into the prepared tin, filling each hollow two-thirds of the way. Bake for 15-20 minutes or until a testing skewer comes out clean when inserted into the centre of the muffins.

Serve with butter.

Makes about 12 muffins.

Cheese spread muffins

Mrs Grace Mofokeng of Sebokeng sent in this recipe. The muffins are deliciously light and may be served with extra cheese spread or grated cheese.

- 550 ml (2⅕ c) cake flour
- 20 ml (4 t) baking powder
- 2 ml (½ t) salt
- 30 ml (2 T) sugar
- 225 ml (⅘ c plus 5 t) milk
- 1 egg
- 60 ml (¼ c) melted butter
- 125 ml (½ c) cheese spread

Preheat the oven to 200 °C (400 °F). Spray a muffin tin with 12 hollows with nonstick spray or grease well with butter or margarine.

Sift the dry ingredients together in a mixing bowl. Add the sugar and mix.

Lightly beat the milk, egg and butter together. Add to dry ingredients, mixing lightly. Add cheese spread and mix. Fill the hollows of the muffin tin two-thirds of the way and bake for 15-20 minutes or until a testing skewer comes out

clean when inserted into the centre of the muffins.

Serve with extra cheese spread or grated cheese.

Makes about 12 muffins.

The Barnyard's spinach muffins

A muffin from the Barnyard farmstall in Tokai, Cape Town is a meal in itself. We tested this recipe in shallow muffin tins and as a result it yielded a bigger batch.

- 6 x 250 ml (6 c) cake flour
- 45 ml (3 T) baking powder
- 15 ml (1 T) salt
- 10 ml (2 t) mixed herbs
- 750 ml (3 c) grated Cheddar cheese
- 2 bunches (300 g each) spinach, finely chopped, boiled and most of the liquid squeezed out
- 300 g margarine, melted
- 250 ml (1 c) milk
- 250 ml (1 c) water
- 6 eggs, whisked

Preheat the oven to 180 °C (350 °F). Spray a few muffin tins with nonstick spray or grease well with butter or margarine.

Sift the dry ingredients together into a large mixing bowl. Add the cheese and spinach and mix. Add the remaining ingredients.

Fill the hollows of the muffin tins three-quarters of the way and bake for about 20-25 minutes or until a testing skewer comes out clean when inserted into the centre of the muffins. Add a little extra water, about 100 ml (⅖ c), to the remaining batter if it has to wait until you make the next batch, as the mixture thickens while standing.

Makes 47 medium muffins.

Gluten-free muffins

Alta Snyman of Kraaifontein, who is allergic to the gluten in wheat flour, sent us a selection of recipes with mealie meal and oats. Ring the changes by varying the ingredients for this muffin recipe.

MUFFINS
- 250 ml (1 c) oats
- 150 ml (⅗ c) instant mealie meal
- 50 ml (⅕ c) margarine
- 100 ml (⅖ c) boiling water
- 180 ml (¾ c) buttermilk or sour milk
- 5 ml (1 t) bicarbonate of soda
- 1 egg
- 80 ml (⅓ c) brown sugar
- 100 ml (⅖ c) cornflour
- 2 ml (½ t) salt

VARIATIONS
- 200 ml (⅘ c) seedless raisins
- 150 ml (⅗ c) sunflower seeds
- 150 ml (⅗ c) chopped nuts
- 200 ml (⅘ c) grated apple

Preheat the oven to 220 °C (425 °F). Spray two muffin tins with nonstick spray or grease well with butter or margarine.

Combine the oats and mealie meal and add the margarine and boiling water. Mix well and leave for a while.

Blend 50 ml (⅕ c) of the buttermilk with the bicarbonate of soda and leave for a while. Beat the egg with remaining buttermilk and brown sugar. Add the buttermilk mixture to the mealie-meal mixture and stir in the bicarbonate of soda mixture. Finally add the cornflour and salt and mix well.

Add one or more of the variations to the muffin batter: raisins and sunflower seeds, or nuts and apple make a delicious combination. Mix and turn into the prepared tins, filling each hollow two-thirds of the way. Bake for about 20 minutes or until done. Cool slightly in the tins before turning out onto a wire rack.

Serve with butter.

Makes about 16 muffins.

Flour-free muffins

Ria Lewis of Messina is sensitive to flour so, in desperation, she devised this muffin recipe. The muffins contain no flour but do include wheat products such as All Bran Flakes and bran. The muffins freeze well, writes Ria.

- 4 x 250 ml plus 125 ml (4½ c) bran
- 200 ml (⅘ c) raisins
- 375 ml (1½ c) boiling water
- 200 ml (⅘ c) melted margarine
- 375 ml (1½ c) oats
- 250 ml (1 c) coconut
- 250 ml (1 c) All Bran Flakes
- 5 ml (1 t) salt
- 375 ml (1½ c) sugar
- 2 extra-large eggs
- 500 ml (2 c) buttermilk
- 560 ml (2¼ c) cornflour
- 15 ml (1 T) bicarbonate of soda
- little milk

Preheat the oven to 200 °C (400 °F). Spray the hollows of a few muffin tins with nonstick spray or grease well with butter or margarine.

Combine the bran and raisins and pour over the boiling water. Add the melted margarine and leave the mixture to cool.

Combine the coconut, All Bran Flakes, salt and sugar.

Whisk the eggs and buttermilk together. Blend the cornflour with a little of the mixture to make a smooth paste. Add the cornflour paste to the remaining buttermilk mixture, mixing well. Blend the bicarbonate of soda with a little milk and add to the buttermilk mixture. Mix with the dry ingredients. Add the margarine mixture. (The batter will be fairly slack.)

Fill the hollows of the muffin tins three-quarters of the way and bake for about 25 minutes or until a testing skewer comes out clean when inserted into the centre of the muffins.

Serve hot or cold with butter.

Makes about 45 muffins.

Superb scones

Scones were one of my first attempts at baking when I was still a youngster and barely tall enough to reach into a mixing bowl. To this day scones are one of my favourite standbys, whether served for breakfast or tea. And ready mixes are a real boon when you're in a hurry – simply vary the ingredients for a different taste every time.
Plain scones taste delicious with the addition of fresh rosemary and a sprinkling of coarse salt on top. Or try a sprinkling of mixed seeds over a round scone loaf. Make the ready mix beforehand and store in the fridge until needed.

Versatile scone ready mix

Ready mix (1)

The recipe for this ready mix was sent in by Mrs Irene Immelman of Ficksburg.

- 7 x 250 ml (7 c) cake flour
- 10 ml (2 t) salt
- 45 ml (3 T) baking powder
- 350 g margarine, cut into pieces

Sift the dry ingredients in a mixing bowl and transfer to the food processor. Add the margarine and process well until the mixture resembles fine mealie meal or breadcrumbs. Spoon into airtight containers and store in the fridge until needed.
Makes about 2,875 litres.

Basic scones (1)

Excellent on their own, or try one of the variations if preferred (see recipes, pp. 54-59).

- 375 ml (1½ c) ready mix (see recipe, above)
- 125 ml (½ c) cake flour
- 5 ml (1 t) baking powder
- about 125 ml (½ c) milk

Preheat the oven to 220 °C (425 °F). Spray a baking sheet with nonstick spray or grease well with butter or margarine.
Mix the ready mix, cake flour and baking powder in a mixing bowl. Add just enough milk to make a dough that rolls out easily and cut in with a knife until just blended.
Roll out on a floured surface until about 2 cm thick. Cut out the scones and arrange on the baking sheet. Bake for about 10 minutes or until done.
Makes about 12 scones.

Cheese puffs

Add Cheddar cheese and a pinch of cayenne pepper to the scone ready mix to make delicious cheese puffs.

- 375 ml (1½ c) scone ready mix (see recipe, left)
- 1 ml (¼ t) salt
- 5 ml (1 t) baking powder
- pinch cayenne pepper
- 250 ml (1 c) grated Cheddar cheese
- 125 ml (½ c) milk

Preheat the oven to 220 °C (425 °F). Spray a muffin tin with nonstick spray or grease well with margarine or butter.
Mix the ready mix, salt, baking powder and cayenne pepper. Add the cheese and mix. Add the milk and mix with a knife to form a soft dough.
Drop spoonfuls of the dough into the hollows of the prepared tin. Bake for about 10-12 minutes or until the crust is golden brown on top.
Serve hot with extra cheese.
Makes 10 cheese puffs.

Ready mix (1)

Scone variations

Scones with spinach, feta and sun-dried tomatoes

A delectable savoury variation.

- 1 x recipe basic scone dough
(see recipe, p. 53, but do not add the milk)
- 100 ml (⅖ c) milk
- 150 g spinach, hard stems removed
and finely chopped
- 8 sun-dried tomatoes in olive oil vinaigrette,
finely chopped
- 50 g feta cheese, crumbled

Preheat the oven to 220 °C (425 °F). Spray a baking sheet with nonstick spray or grease well with butter or margarine.

Prepare the scone dough as described in the basic scone recipe, but do not add the milk.

Cook the spinach until tender and drain well by pressing out the water through a sieve. Add the drained spinach, sun-dried tomatoes and feta cheese to the basic dry scone mixture and mix.

Mix in the 100 ml (⅖ c) milk with a knife until just blended. Roll out the dough on a floured surface until about 2 cm thick. Cut out circles, 5,5 cm in diameter.

Arrange on the prepared baking sheet and bake for about 15-20 minutes until done or the crust is golden brown on top.

Serve hot with butter and feta cheese if preferred.
Makes 10-11 scones.

Scones with coarse salt and rosemary

Something different for tea time.

- 1 x recipe basic scone dough
(see recipe, p. 53)
- olive oil
- 3-5 ml (generous ½-1 t) coarse salt
- 10 ml (2 t) fresh rosemary (broken into sprigs)

Preheat the oven to 220 °C (425 °F). Spray a baking sheet with nonstick spray or grease well with butter or margarine.

Prepare the scone dough as described in the basic scone recipe.

Roll out the dough on a floured surface until about 2 cm thick. Cut out circles, 5,5 cm in diameter, and arrange on the prepared baking sheet.

Brush with the olive oil and sprinkle with the coarse salt and rosemary. Bake for about 10 minutes until done

and the crust is golden brown.

Serve hot with olives and feta cheese in olive oil and a dash of lemon juice if preferred.
Makes 10 scones.

Round seed scone loaf

Easy, economical and delicious.

- 1 x recipe basic scone dough (see recipe, p. 53)
- variety seeds such as linseeds, sesame seeds,
poppy seeds and sunflower seeds

Preheat the oven to 220 °C (425 °F). Spray a baking sheet with nonstick spray or grease well with butter or margarine.

Prepare the scone dough as described in the recipe for the basic scones. Shape the dough into a round, 2-cm-thick loaf. Place on the prepared baking sheet. Divide the round loaf into segments with a knife.

Sprinkle different seeds onto each segment. Bake for about 10-15 minutes until done and golden brown.

Serve hot with butter.
Makes a small loaf.

Olive rounds

It looks impressive and tastes delicious.

- 1 x recipe basic scone dough (see recipe, p. 53)
- 20 ml (4 t) olive oil
- 5 black olives, stoned and quartered
- 15 ml (1 T) fresh rosemary leaves
- 15 ml (1 T) coarse salt
- olive oil for brushing on top

Preheat the oven to 220 °C (425 °F). Spray a deep muffin tin with nonstick spray or grease well with butter or margarine.

Roll out the scone dough into a rectangle, about 1 cm thick. Brush the dough lightly with olive oil, lightly press olives and rosemary into the dough and sprinkle with coarse salt. Roll up the dough as for a Swiss roll and cut into 3-cm-thick slices.

Arrange the slices in the prepared hollows of the muffin tin, brush lightly with olive oil and sprinkle with leftover rosemary and coarse salt. Bake for 10-12 minutes until done or golden brown.

Makes 10-12 rounds.

Olive rounds

Herbed scone roll

A scone roll with a herb filling.

- 2 x recipes basic scone dough (see recipe, p. 53)

HERB FILLING
- 125 ml (½ c) freshly chopped herbs such as chives, origanum, thyme, sage and parsley
- 2 cloves garlic, crushed
- ½ packet (50 g) ground almonds
- 50 g Parmesan cheese
- 150 ml (⅗ c) olive oil
- black pepper to taste

Preheat the oven to 200 °C (400 °F). Spray a baking sheet with nonstick spray or grease well with butter or margarine.

■ HERB FILLING: Place all the filling ingredients in the food processor and chop finely to form a paste.

Prepare the scone dough as described in the basic scone recipe. On a floured surface, roll out the dough into a rectangle about 1 cm thick. Spread with the herb mixture until completely covered and roll up lengthwise. Place on the greased baking sheet.

Bake for about 20 minutes or until done and golden brown on top.

Serve with the leftover herb mixture.

Makes 1 herbed scone roll.

Herbed scone roll

Garlic and chilli scone ring

This scone ring tastes divine served with a garlic sauce.

- 2 x recipes basic scone dough (see recipe, p. 53)

GARLIC SAUCE
- 200 g butter
- 10 ml (2 t) cayenne pepper
- 3 cloves garlic, crushed
- 5 ml (1 t) garlic salt
- 25 ml (5 t) finely chopped fresh parsley

Preheat the oven to 200 °C (400 °F). Spray a 20-cm loose-bottomed ring tin with nonstick spray or grease well with butter or margarine.

- GARLIC SAUCE: Place all the sauce ingredients in a glass mixing bowl and microwave for a few minutes on 100 per cent power or until the butter has melted.

Prepare the scone dough as described in the basic scone recipe. Roll the dough out on a floured surface until about 2 cm thick. Cut out circles, 5,5 cm in diameter.

Dip the circles in the sauce and pack fairly tightly in the prepared ring tin. Place the ring tin on a baking sheet and bake for about 35 minutes until done or golden brown.

Serve hot with the remaining sauce.

Makes a medium loaf.

Scone ready mix

Ready mix (2)

This ready mix can be stored in the fridge for up to four weeks.

- 9 x 250 ml (9 c) cake flour
- 225 ml (⅘ c plus 5 t) low-fat milk powder
- 50 ml (10 t) baking powder
- 10 ml (2 t) salt
- 250 g butter, diced

In a large mixing bowl, sift together all the dry ingredients. Add the diced butter and rub it in with your fingertips until the mixture resembles dried breadcrumbs. Spoon into airtight containers. The mixture keeps well in the fridge for about four weeks.

Makes 6 batches of about 7 scones each.

Basic scones (2)

This is an even easier scone recipe.

- 410 ml (1⅔ c) basic ready mix (see recipe, left)
- 125 ml (½ c) ice-cold water
- milk for brushing on top

Preheat the oven to 220 °C (425 °F). Spray a baking sheet with nonstick spray or grease well with butter or margarine.

Lightly mix the ice-cold water into the prepared mixture with a knife until just blended. Roll out on a floured surface until 1,5 cm thick. Cut out circles or any other shapes, 6-7 cm in diameter.

Arrange 2 cm apart on the baking sheet and brush on top with a little milk.

Bake for 12-15 minutes or until the scones are nicely browned on top.

Serve hot with butter, honey, cheese or jam.

Makes 7-8 scones.

■ Variations

■ **Sweet scones:** Combine 410 ml (1⅔ c) ready mix with 125 ml (½ c) currants and 15 ml (1 T) sugar. Add 125 ml (½ c) ice-cold water and proceed as described in the basic scone recipe. Makes 8 scones.

■ **Cheese scones:** Combine 410 ml (1⅔ c) ready mix with 125 ml (½ c) grated Cheddar cheese and 1 ml (¼ t) cayenne pepper. Add 125 ml (½ c) ice-cold water and proceed as described in the basic scone recipe. Makes 8 scones.

■ **Herbed scones:** Combine 410 ml (1⅔ c) ready mix with 60 ml (¼ c) chopped fresh herbs (such as parsley, dill and basil) and add 125 ml (½ c) ice-cold water. Proceed as described in the basic scone recipe. Makes 8 scones.

Garlic and chilli scone ring

More ideas with scones

Sesame seed scones

Mrs Vicky van Schalkwyk of Arcadia sent us this variation on ordinary scones.

- 500 ml (2 c) self-raising flour
- 2 ml (½ t) salt
- 30 ml (2 T) sugar
- 100 ml (⅖ c) sesame seeds
- 70 g butter
- 1 egg, lightly whisked
- 125 ml (½ c) sour cream
- whisked egg yolk for brushing on top
- extra sesame seeds for sprinkling on top

Preheat the oven to 200 °C (400 °F). Spray a baking sheet with nonstick spray or grease well with butter or margarine.

Sift the self-raising flour and salt together. Add the sugar and sesame seeds and mix lightly. Grate in the butter and rub in with your fingertips until the mixture resembles breadcrumbs. Add the whisked egg and sour cream, mixing gently with a spatula until just blended.

On a lightly floured surface, roll out the dough until 2,5 cm thick. Cut out circles 6-7 cm in diameter and arrange on the prepared baking sheet. Brush with egg yolk and sprinkle with extra sesame seeds. Bake for 20 minutes or until done and golden brown on top.

Makes 12-15 scones.

Pumpkin scone wheel

Mock croissants

These mock croissants are quick to make with scone dough.

- 900 ml (3⅗ c) cake flour
- 25 ml (5 t) baking powder
- 2 ml (½ t) salt
- 1 ml (¼ t) cayenne pepper
- 125 g butter or margarine
- 200 g (500 ml) Cheddar cheese, grated
- 300-325 ml (1⅕-1¼ c) milk
- 1 egg yolk

Preheat the oven to 200 °C (400 °F). Spray a baking sheet with nonstick spray or grease well with butter or margarine.

Sift the dry ingredients together and rub in the butter with your fingertips until the mixture resembles breadcrumbs. Add the cheese and about 275-300 ml milk to form a stiff dough that can be rolled out.

Divide the dough into four equal portions. Roll each quarter into a thin round 20 cm in diameter.

Trim the outer edge of each round and divide into eight uniform wedges. Roll up each wedge, starting at the outer edge. Shape the rolls into half-moons and arrange on a greased baking sheet, allowing sufficient space in between.

Whisk the egg yolk and remaining 25 ml (5 t) milk and brush the rolls with the mixture. Place the rolls in the top of the oven and bake for about 15 minutes or until golden brown.

Makes 32 croissants.

Pumpkin scone wheel

Tilla Kleu of Somerset East makes a tasty scone wheel using cooked pumpkin.

- 300 ml (1⅕ c) cake flour
- 150 ml (⅗ c) mealie meal
- 30 ml (2 T) caster sugar
- 3 ml (generous ½ t) ground ginger
- 3 ml (generous ½ t) salt
- 17 ml (heaped tablespoon) baking powder
- 10 ml (2 t) ground cinnamon
- 100 g butter
- 100 ml (⅖ c) seedless raisins
- 375 ml (1½ c) cooked pumpkin, pressed through a sieve
- melted butter to brush on top (optional)
- 15 ml (1 T) sugar (optional)
- 2 ml (½ t) ground cinnamon (optional)

Preheat the oven to 220 °C (440 °F). Spray a baking sheet with nonstick spray or grease well with butter or margarine.

Sift the dry ingredients together and rub in the butter with your fingertips until well blended. Add the raisins and pumpkin and mix with a fork until just blended.

Divide the dough in half, shape each half into a circle about 15 cm in diameter and place on the baking sheet. Lightly mark eight wedges with a knife. Brush with melted butter, if preferred. Combine the sugar and cinnamon and sprinkle over, if preferred.

Bake for about 10 minutes or until done.

Makes 16 wedges.

Sunflower scones

These scones look like sunflowers. The dough is shaped into a sunflower and sprinkled with sunflower seeds.

- 400 ml (1⅗ c) cake flour
- 500 ml (2 c) whole-wheat flour
- 15 ml (1 T) baking powder
- 5 ml (1 t) salt
- 90 g soft butter
- 300-350 ml (1⅕-1⅖ c) sour milk
- egg yolk for brushing on top
- 30 ml (2 T) sunflower seeds

Preheat the oven to 200 °C (400 °F). Spray a baking sheet with nonstick spray or grease well with butter or margarine.

In a mixing bowl, sift together the cake flour, whole-wheat flour, baking powder and salt. Add the bran left behind in the sieve to the bowl. Rub in the butter with your fingertips until well blended and the mixture resembles breadcrumbs. Add the sour milk, mixing lightly to form a soft dough. Do not overmix. (Add more cake flour if the dough sticks to your hands.)

Divide the dough into three equal portions. Shape into three balls and place on the prepared baking sheet. Use a glass to press a circle in the centre of each ball.

With a sharp knife, make fairly deep cuts from the glass to the edge of the circle to make a flower pattern. Brush with egg yolk and sprinkle sunflower seeds in the centre of each "flower". Bake for 25 minutes or until done and golden brown.

Serve lukewarm with butter and cheese.

Makes 12 scones.

Pizzas with pizzazz

Tired of boring pizzas with cheese and tomato? Here are some interesting ideas for pizza toppings with a difference. They're all quick and versatile. Pizzas are great as a main course, side dish or snack with drinks. If you're hard-pressed for time, make them on the stove plate. And don't forget to try the baking-sheet, pan and bread pizzas.

Basic pizza dough

Enough for two to three pizzas, but halve the recipe if you want to make only one. Any leftover dough will keep for up to one week in the fridge for later use – but remember to knock it back occasionally.

- 4 x 250 ml (4 c) cake flour
- 5 ml (1 t) salt
- 7 ml (1 ½ t) instant yeast
- 30 ml (2 T) olive oil
- about 300 ml (1 ⅕ c) lukewarm water
- olive oil for sprinkling on top

Preheat the oven to 200 °C (400 °F). Spray two to three baking sheets with nonstick spray or grease well with butter or magarine.

Combine the cake flour and salt in a large mixing bowl. Sprinkle the instant yeast on top and pour over the olive oil. Mix lightly with a knife. Add just enough lukewarm water to form a soft, manageable dough and mix by hand while adding the 300 ml (⅘ c) lukewarm water.

Knead for about 10 minutes or until the dough is smooth and elastic. Cover lightly with a sheet of oiled plastic wrap and leave to rise for 20 minutes in a warm place. Divide the dough in two to three uniform pieces and knock back. On a floured surface, roll out circles about 5-7 mm thick.

Arrange the dough circles on the prepared baking sheets and cover with a topping of your choice. Sprinkle with a little olive oil if preferred, and leave to rise in a warm place until double in volume.

Bake for about 15-20 minutes or until the pizza crust is done. (If you prefer a crisp crust, leave the dough to rise without the topping and bake as is for about 5 minutes before adding the topping.)

Makes 2-3 pizza bases.

Pizza toppings

- **Sage and feta cheese:** Brush one rolled out dough circle with a little olive oil. Arrange 15-20 whole or chopped fresh sage leaves and 125-150 g feta cheese, coarsely crumbled, on the dough and prepare as described. Makes 1 large pizza.
- **Olives, anchovies and capers:** Brush one rolled out dough circle with a little olive oil. Arrange the following ingredients on the dough: 100 g black or green olives, stoned and finely chopped; 2 cloves garlic, crushed; 1 can (50 g) drained anchovy fillets; ½ green chilli, seeded and finely chopped; 1 can (410 g) whole skinned tomatoes, finely chopped and 30 ml (2 T) capers. Prepare as described. Makes 1 large pizza.
- **Onion and tomato:** Thinly slice 2 small red onions and mix with 30 ml (2 T) olive oil and 15 ml (1 T) red wine vinegar. Brush a rolled out dough circle with olive oil and sprinkle the onion slices on top. Slice 1 can (410 g) whole skinned tomatoes and seed, if preferred. Top the pizza with the tomato slices and sprinkle with a little dried basil. Season to taste with salt and freshly ground black pepper, and prepare as described. Makes 1 large pizza.
- **Rosemary and garlic:** Heat 45 ml (3 T) olive oil. Crush or thinly slice 4 cloves garlic. Sauté the garlic and 45 ml (3 T) crushed, fresh or 15 ml (1 T) dried rosemary until the garlic is tender. Spread over the rolled out dough circle, sprinkle with a little coarse salt and prepare as described. Makes 1 large pizza.

Baking-sheet pizza (p. 64)

Baking-sheet pizza

The crust takes only a few minutes to make. Joyce Kirk of Witbank says her guests always rave about this pizza. The topping can be varied as preferred.

CRUST
- 500 ml (2 c) cake flour
- 20 ml (4 t) baking powder
- 5 ml (1 t) mustard powder
- 180 ml (¾ c) oil
- 125 ml (½ c) boiling water

TOPPING
- 1 can (410 g) tomato and onion mix
- 2 cloves garlic, crushed
- 7 ml (1½ t) mixed dried herbs
- 5 ml (1 t) origanum
- salt and freshly ground black pepper
- about 250 ml (1 c) grated Cheddar cheese
- 125 g coctail sausages or Vienna sausages, cut into pieces
- 4-6 small gherkins, cut into fans

Preheat the oven to 190 °C (375 °F). Spray a 24 x 33-cm baking sheet with nonstick spray or grease well with butter or margarine.
- CRUST: Combine all the dry ingredients for the crust and add the oil and water. Mix to form a stiff dough and press into the prepared baking sheet.
- TOPPING: Heat the tomato and onion mix and add the garlic and herbs. Season with salt and pepper and spread over the crust. Sprinkle with a little cheese.

Arrange the sausages and gherkins on top and bake for 25-30 minutes or until done.

Serve hot or cold.

Serves 4-6.

Pan pizza

Mrs Joan O'Neill of Warrenton sent us this recipe after the recipe for the baking-sheet pizza appeared in *You*. It's even quicker and more economical as it's made in a pan on top of the stove – Joan uses the Bauer pan she ordered through *You*.

TOMATO AND ONION MIX
- oil
- 1 onion, thinly sliced
- 1 clove garlic, finely chopped or 2 ml (½ t) garlic flakes
- 2 tomatoes, skinned and coarsely chopped
- 5 ml (1 t) origanum
- 15 ml (1 T) sandwich spread
- salt and freshly ground black pepper

CRUST
- 250 ml (1 c) self-raising flour
- 3 ml (generous ½ t) mustard powder
- 3 ml (generous ½ t) pizza pasta seasoning
- 3 ml (generous ½ t) salt
- 1 ml (¼ t) cayenne pepper
- 1 large egg
- 100 ml (⅖ c) milk

TOPPING
- few mushrooms, halved
- few olives
- about 250 ml (1 c) grated Cheddar cheese

- TOMATO AND ONION MIX: Heat the pan with a little oil. Wipe the pan to remove excess oil and sauté the onion and garlic until tender. Add the tomatoes and simmer until a purée is formed. Season with the origanum, sandwich spread, and salt and pepper to taste. Remove from the pan. Wipe the pan.
- CRUST: Heat the pan with a little oil. Wipe the pan to remove excess oil. Sift self-raising flour and seasonings. Whisk egg and milk and add to dry ingredients. Mix until well blended. Spread evenly over surface of pan.

Heat on the stove plate until cooked and brown underneath, turn the crust and heat the other side until done. Meanwhile spread the tomato and onion mix over the crust and sprinkle with the mushrooms, olives and cheese. Unscrew the wooden handle of the pan and place under the oven grill until the cheese has melted.

Serve hot.

Makes 1 large pizza.

Pizza on top of the stove

Bake this pizza when you're pressed for time.

- olive oil
- ⅓ x recipe for basic pizza dough (see recipe, p. 63)
- any of the toppings (see pizza toppings, p. 63)

Brush the bottom of your largest nonstick pan with olive oil and heat over medium heat.

Roll out the pizza dough until about 3 mm thick and shape so it fits into the bottom of your largest nonstick pan. Place the dough in the pan and heat for about 5-10 minutes or until the bottom is crisp.

Turn over and heat for a further 3-10 minutes until crisp and done. Remove the crust from the pan, brush with extra olive oil, if preferred, and add the topping of your choice.

Place under the preheated oven grill and heat until the topping is just warmed and the cheese melted and golden brown (if used).

Makes 1 large pizza.

Pan pizza

Bread pizza

For an instant pizza that tastes like the real thing, stack any of your favourite pizza toppings on a slice of bread.

- white or brown bread slices
- butter
- canned tomato and onion mix
- choice of topping (see box)
- grated mozzarella cheese for sprinkling on top

Lightly butter the bread slices on one side and arrange on a prepared baking sheet.

Spread with a little tomato and onion mix (the canned type is perfect) and stack with any of the toppings. Sprinkle with grated mozzarella cheese. Switch on the oven grill and grill until the cheese has melted.

Ten ideas for pizza toppings

Pizza 1: diced pineapple and ham

Pizza 2: onion rings, few rashers bacon and avocado slices

Pizza 3: few slices salami, onion rings, strips of green pepper and sliced mushrooms

Pizza 4: sliced mushrooms and strips of fresh garlic

Pizza 5: banana slices and few rashers bacon

Pizza 6: shredded tuna, strips of green pepper and onion rings

Pizza 7: savoury mince and onion rings

Pizza 8: sliced mushrooms and diced ham

Pizza 9: strips of cooked chicken, whole-kernel sweetcorn and strips of green pepper

Pizza 10: fresh tomato slices and gherkins

Vetkoek, griddlecakes, crumpets, pancakes and fritters

Remember the vetkoek and pancakes Grandma used to make? Have you all but forgotten how you used to make stokbrood (bread on a stick) and ashcakes over smouldering coals? Bring back those memories with these recipes – they're easy enough for the youngsters to try out as well. We've also included recipes for crumpets and fritters.

Vetkoek and fillings

Vetkoek

Enjoy old-fashioned vetkoek with butter and syrup, or make a meal of it with a curry filling or braaied sausage smothered in home-made tomato sauce. Alternatively, try our recipes for a mince or pilchard filling.

VETKOEK
- 6 x 250 ml (6 c) cake flour
- 1 packet (10 g) instant yeast
- 10 ml (2 t) salt
- 40 ml (8 t) sugar
- about 1 litre (4 x 250 ml) lukewarm water
- oil for frying

MINCE FILLING
- 1 onion, grated
- 1 green pepper, finely chopped
- 1 clove garlic, crushed
- 25 ml (5 t) oil
- 250 g mince
- 30 ml (2 T) tomato sauce
- 12,5 ml (2½ t) Worcester sauce
- pinch dried thyme
- pinch dried origanum
- salt and freshly ground black pepper
- 15 ml (1 T) cornflour, blended with a little water

PILCHARD FILLING
- 1 onion, finely chopped
- 2 carrots, scraped and sliced into thin strips
- 1 celery stick, chopped into rings
- oil
- 1 can (425 g) pilchards in tomato sauce, flaked
- grated rind and juice of 1 lemon
- 2 ml (½ t) mixed dried herbs
- salt and black pepper to taste

■ VETKOEK: Sift together the dry ingredients. Add just enough lukewarm water to form a fairly slack dough and mix well. Cover with greased plastic wrap and leave in the mixing bowl to rise until double in volume.

Heat sufficient oil in a pan. Fry tablespoonfuls of dough until golden brown on the outside and cooked inside. Drain on paper towelling.

Makes about 35 vetkoeke.

■ MINCE FILLING: Sauté the onion, green pepper and garlic in heated oil until tender. Add small quantities of the mince at a time and fry until done but not brown. Add the tomato sauce, Worcester sauce and seasonings. Stir in the cornflour and heat until the mixture thickens slightly. Cut the vetkoek open halfway and spoon a little of the filling into the hollows.

Enough for about 20 vetkoeke.

■ PILCHARD FILLING: Sauté the onion, carrots and celery in a little oil until tender. Add the pilchards in tomato sauce and season with the lemon juice and rind, mixed herbs, and salt and black pepper to taste. Simmer for 5 minutes. Cut the vetkoek open halfway and spoon a little of the filling into the hollows.

Enough for about 30 vetkoeke.

Mealie-meal vetkoek (p. 68)

Mealie-meal vetkoek

Mrs L. Jonker of Newcastle makes these vetkoek with leftover mealie-meal porridge. The recipe is ideal for people who're allergic to wheat or milk as it contains neither.

- 500-750 ml (2-3 c) left over mealie-meal porridge or 500 ml (2 c) mealie meal
- 500 ml (2 c) water
- 5 ml (1 t) salt
- 2 extra-large eggs, whisked
- 60 ml (¼ c) cornflour
- 5 ml (1 t) baking powder
- pinch salt
- 1 can (420 g) cream-style sweetcorn
- oil for deep frying

Use left over mealie-meal porridge or blend the mealie meal with a little water until smooth. Bring the remaining water and salt to the boil. Add the mealie meal paste, mixing well. Bring to the boil while stirring continuously and simmer for about 10-15 minutes until cooked. Cool slightly.

Add the whisked egg to the stiff porridge and mix well. Sift in the cornflour, baking powder and salt. Add the sweetcorn and mix well.

Drop spoonfuls of the batter into heated oil for deep frying. Fry until golden brown on the outside and cooked inside. Drain on paper towelling.

Serve as is or with margarine and honey for a delicious snack, or serve as a side dish.

Makes 25 vetkoeke.

Rekkenbekke

Rekkenbekke are vetkoek that are not prepared in deep oil. Ettie Maritz of White River flavours hers with cheese, fresh herbs or garlic.

- 625 ml (2½ c) cake flour
- 20 ml (4 t) baking powder
- pinch salt
- 1 extra-large egg, whisked
- about 350 ml (1⅖ c) milk
- 25 ml (5 t) grated Cheddar cheese
- 5 ml (1 t) fresh herbs of your choice
- 5 ml (1 t) crushed garlic
- oil for frying

Sift the cake flour, baking powder and salt together. Add the egg and small quantities of the milk, stirring continuously until a stiff batter is formed. Divide the mixture into three equal parts and add the cheese to one part, herbs to the second and garlic to the third.

Heat a Bauer pan (or ordinary pan), lightly brushed with oil, and drop spoonfuls of the mixture into the pan. Fry until golden brown on the outside and cooked inside.

Serve hot with butter.

Makes 9 rekkenbekke.

Onion vetkoek

Mrs Elfriede Bezuidenhout of aMmabele says this onion vetkoek is excellent with braaied meat.

- 2 ml (½ t) salt
- 2 ml (½ t) seasoning (such as Aromat)
- 5 eggs, whisked
- 800 ml (3⅕ c) self-raising flour
- 125 ml (½ c) water
- 3 onions, finely chopped
- oil for frying

Add the seasonings to the eggs and sift in the self-raising flour. Add the water and mix well. Add the chopped onions and stir until well blended.

Heat sufficient oil in a pan and drop spoonfuls of the batter in the oil. Fry until golden brown on the outside and cooked inside.

Makes 12-15 vetkoeke.

Paul's sweetcorn vetkoek

When the kids become bored with sandwiches, these small vetkoeke make a delicious change. Mrs Gertie van Zyl of Wright Park, Springs, often makes them for her children's school lunch boxes.

- 250 ml (1 c) self-raising flour
- 5 ml (1 t) salt
- 1 can (420 g) cream-style sweetcorn
- 500 ml (2 c) cold water
- oil for frying

Combine the self-raising flour, salt and sweetcorn in a mixing bowl. Add the water and mix to form a fairly slack batter.

Heat sufficient oil in a shallow pan. Drop spoonfuls of the batter in the oil and fry until nicely browned on the outside and done inside.

Makes 30 vetkoeke.

Rekkenbekke

Stokbrood and griddlecakes

Stokbrood (bread on a stick)

Wrap dough around a stick and cook over hot coals until done – kids especially love making their own stokbrood. Fill the hollows left by the stick with butter and syrup.

- 1 kg cake flour
- 5 ml (1 t) salt
- 2 packets (10 g each) instant yeast
- 125 g butter or margarine
- 250 ml (1 c) buttermilk
- 400-500 ml (1⅗-2 c) lukewarm water

Sift together the cake flour and salt. Sprinkle the instant yeast on top and mix. Rub in the butter with your fingertips until well blended.

Add the buttermilk and mix. Add just enough water to form a stiff dough. Knead until smooth and elastic and until the dough no longer sticks to your hands. Cover the dough and leave in a warm place for about 30 minutes. Knock back and divide the dough into 12 uniform pieces. Roll each piece of dough into a roll 20-25 cm long and wrap in a spiral around 12 green sticks.

Leave to rise a little in a warm place. Slowly cook the stokbrode over the coals until done. Remove the sticks and fill the hollows with butter and syrup.

Makes 12 stokbrode.

Griddlecakes

The members of the women's agricultural organisation in Vanrhynsdorp use this recipe to make griddlecakes.

- 1 kg white bread flour
- 7 ml (1½ t) sugar
- 2 ml (½ t) salt
- 1 packet (10 g) instant yeast
- 500-600 ml (2-2⅖ c) lukewarm water
- 15 ml (1 T) melted butter or margarine
- flour for sprinkling on top

Combine the flour, sugar, salt and instant yeast. Add just enough lukewarm water to form a stiff dough. Knead well until the dough is smooth and elastic and no longer sticks to your hands. Brush the dough with melted butter or margarine and cover.

Leave the dough in a warm place to rise until double in volume. Knock back and shape into 12-15 balls. Flatten slightly and sprinkle a little flour over each cake. Leave to rise until double in volume. Cook over slow coals until done.

Makes 12-15 griddlecakes.

> ■ **Ashcakes:** This recipe will really take you back to your childhood days. Prepare 1 x recipe griddlecakes (see recipe above), but make the balls slightly larger. Leave to rise a little and place the cakes in the hot ash (not in the coals). Cover the cakes with ash and leave for about 30 minutes before removing. Knock the ashcakes together to get rid of most of the ash.
>
> ■ **Potbread:** Grease a flat-bottomed cast-iron pot, 28 cm in diameter and 10 cm deep, with butter or margarine. Also grease the lid. Prepared 1 x recipe for griddlecakes (see recipe above). Knock back the dough after it has risen the first time, shape into a round bread and place in the cast-iron pot. Cover with the lid and leave to rise again until the bread nearly fills the pot. Bake for about 40-60 minutes in a preheated oven at 190 °C (375 °F). Alternatively, dig a hole in the ground and fill with a few coals. Arrange rocks or bricks on top, place the cast-iron pot on top and place a few coals on the lid. Bake the bread for 40-60 minutes or until done.

Crumpets

Crumpets

Crumpets are a great standby when you've run out of bread or to have for breakfast. Enjoy them with honey or golden syrup or add any of the variations and serve with cheese.

CRUMPETS
- 250 ml (1 c) self-raising flour
- 2 ml (½ t) bicarbonate of soda
- pinch salt
- 200-300 ml (⅘-1⅕ c) plain yoghurt, buttermilk or sour milk
- 1 extra-large egg
- 15 ml (1 T) melted butter
- oil

VARIATIONS
- chopped green pepper
- sweetcorn
- finely chopped onion and parsley

CRUMPETS: Sift together the dry ingredients.

Whisk the yoghurt and egg together and add the melted butter. Add the dry ingredients and stir with a whisk until smooth. Add any of the variations if preferred.

Drop tablespoonfuls of the batter in a preheated pan which has been lightly brushed with oil. Heat until air bubbles form on the surface, turn and heat until golden brown on the other side.

Serve with golden syrup, honey and grated cheese. Makes 10 crumpets.

From bottom left, clockwise: Griddlecakes, Stokbrood and Ashcakes

Sweetcorn crumpets with yoghurt sauce

Serve these crumpets for breakfast with this special yoghurt sauce. Ideal for an outdoor breakfast, in which case the crumpets can be made on a gas braai.

CRUMPETS
- 300 g cooked sweetcorn kernels, finely chopped
- 150 ml (⅗ c) thick cream
- 150 ml (⅗ c) cake flour
- 1 onion, chopped
- 4 eggs, separated
- 5 ml (1 t) salt
- 1 ml (¼ t) freshly ground black pepper
- 5 ml (1 t) fresh or 2 ml (½ t) dried parsley
- oil

YOGHURT SAUCE
- 200 ml (⅘ c) plain yoghurt
- 50 ml (⅕ c) mayonnaise
- 50 ml (⅕ c) sour cream
- 20 ml (4 t) chopped chives
- pinch freshly ground black pepper
- 5 ml (1 t) lemon juice

■ YOGHURT SAUCE: Mix all the ingredients for the sauce and chill until needed.

■ CRUMPETS: Mix the sweetcorn with the cream, cake flour, onion, egg yolks, salt, pepper and parsley. Whisk the egg whites until stiff and fold into the mixture.

Brush the smooth side of a Grillogas braai or skottelbraai with oil and heat. Drop spoonfuls of the mixture onto the surface and fry until golden brown on one side, turn and repeat on the other side. (The crumpets may also be baked in an electric frying pan.)

Serve with the yoghurt sauce. Alternatively, omit the onion and parsley and serve with butter and honey.

Makes about 10 crumpets.

Sweetcorn crumpets with yoghurt sauce

Maltabella crumpets

These crumpets are delicious served with stewed dried fruit.

- 500 ml (2 c) Maltabella flour
- 10 ml (2 t) bicarbonate of soda
- pinch salt
- 10 ml (2 t) molasses or brown sugar
- 20 ml (4 t) melted butter
- 375 ml (1½ c) plain yoghurt or amaas
- oil

Sift together the flour, bicarbonate of soda and salt in a mixing bowl. Add the molasses, butter and yoghurt to the dry ingredients and mix.

Heat a little oil in a Bauer pan. Wipe the pan with paper towelling to remove any excess oil. Drop spoonfuls of the mixture in the pan and heat until air bubbles form on the surface. Turn and heat until cooked on the other side. Serve with stewed dried fruit and plain yoghurt, or with golden syrup or honey and cheese.

Makes about 20 crumpets.

Pancakes

Bulk recipe for pancakes

Her mother works in a shop where they make the most delicious pancakes, writes Miss A. Pruis of Witbank. The batter keeps in the fridge for two to three days. The pancakes do not become tough when reheated.

- 5 extra-large eggs
- 1,5 litres (6 x 250 ml) milk
- 5 ml (1 t) salt
- 500 ml (2 c) oil
- 15 ml (1 T) vanilla essence
- 4 x 250 ml (4 c) self-raising flour

Whisk together the eggs, milk, salt and oil. Add the vanilla essence. Add small quantities of the self-raising flour at a time, mixing well after each addition. Beat well until the mixture is smooth and lump-free. Leave for at least 30 minutes.

Spray a 15-cm pan with nonstick spray or brush with oil. Heat the pan and add just enough batter to cover the base. Bake until done on both sides. Serve with cinnamon sugar and lemon slices.

Makes 40-50 pancakes.

Basic pancake batter

Winter is perfect pancake weather. Freshly baked and rolled up with a generous sprinkling of cinnamon sugar inside, pancakes will help you forget about the cold outside. Make a large batch of batter and keep in the fridge for two to three days so you can bake delicious pancakes whenever you feel like it. Alternatively, bake an entire batch of pancakes, stack them with layers of plastic wrap in between and freeze for up to two months.

- 375 ml (1½ c) cake flour
- 1 ml (¼ t) salt
- 5 ml (1 t) baking powder
- 500 ml (2 c) water
- 1 extra-large egg
- 7 ml (1½ t) vinegar
- 15 ml (1 T) oil
- oil for frying

Sift together the dry ingredients three times and make a hollow in the centre. Whisk the water, egg, vinegar and oil together and gradually add the mixture to the dry ingredients while beating with a wooden spoon or electric beater, or in the food processor. Leave the batter to rest for at least 30 minutes and bake as follows: Brush a 15-cm pan with a little oil, heat well and wipe the pan with paper towelling to remove any excess oil.

Pour just enough batter in the pan to cover the base. Tilt the pan from side to side to ensure the entire base is covered.

Heat until the sides of the pancake shrink slightly from the pan. Turn the pancake with an egg flip. Heat until cooked and pale brown. Turn out onto a plate. Repeat with the remaining batter. Fill as preferred (see ideas for fillings, p. 77), or sprinkle with cinnamon sugar, roll up, arrange on a plate and keep warm over a saucepan with boiling water.

Makes about 15 pancakes.

Bulk recipe for pancakes

Pancake fillings and ideas

Dried pears and aniseed filling

Mrs Jennifer-Lynn Sprawson of Rooseveldt Park loves spoiling her family with pancakes. She even fills them with mince and tops them with a cheese sauce for a light meal. This filling makes wonderful dessert pancakes.

- 250 g dried pears, coarsely chopped and cooked in rooibos tea until tender
- 7 ml (1½ t) aniseed
- 50 ml (⅕ c) caster sugar
- 30 ml (2 T) butter
- 25 ml (5 t) rum

Drain the pears slightly and mix with the remaining ingredients. Heat until warmed through and spoon on top of the pancakes. Roll up and serve with cream and a sprinkling of cinnamon sugar if preferred.
Enough for 12-15 pancakes.

Apple filling

Another recipe for a sweet pancake filling sent in by Mrs Jennifer-Lynn Sprawson of Rooseveldt Park.

APPLE FILLING
- 3 large green apples, peeled, cored and thinly sliced
- 125 ml (½ c) sugar
- 100 ml (⅖ c) raisins
- 5 ml (1 t) ground cinnamon
- 2 whole cloves
- 15 ml (1 T) lemon juice
- enough water to cover the apple slices
- 25 ml (5 t) butter
- 15 ml (1 T) custard powder, blended with a little water
- 30 ml (2 T) brandy

CINNAMON CREAM
- 250 ml (1 c) cream, stiffly whipped
- 50 ml (⅕ c) caster sugar
- 5 ml (1 t) ground cinnamon

- APPLE FILLING: Place the apples, sugar, raisins, cinnamon, cloves and lemon juice in a saucepan and add just enough water to cover the apple slices.
  Bring to the boil and simmer until the apple slices are just tender. Add the butter and thicken the mixture with the custard powder paste.
  Bring to the boil once more and add the brandy. Fill the pancakes with the apple filling.
- CINNAMON CREAM: Mix all the ingredients for the cinnamon cream and serve with the pancakes.
  Enough for about 15 pancakes.

Pancake sandwiches

Stale bread can be used in all kinds of ways. Mrs I.A. du Plessis of Parow makes apricot sandwiches, dips them in pancake batter, and fries them in oil. Sprinkled with cinnamon sugar, they're delicious.

- 6 slices day-old white bread
- smooth apricot jam
- little milk
- pancake batter (see recipe for pancake batter, p. 74)
- enough oil for shallow frying
- cinnamon sugar

Spread three slices of bread with a thick layer of apricot jam and sandwich together in twos with the remaining three slices. Quarter each sandwich to make 12 triangles.
Rapidly dip each triangle in a little milk and then in the pancake batter. Fry in shallow oil on both sides until golden brown. Sprinkle with cinnamon sugar while still hot and serve lukewarm.
Makes 12 triangles.

Pancake with Dried pears and aniseed filling

Whole-wheat pancakes

Mrs Marietjie Kotze of Pretoria serves these pancakes with a mushroom or apple filling. The pancake batter is fairly slack, but makes perfect pancakes.

PANCAKES
- 500 ml (2 c) whole-wheat flour
- 10 ml (2 t) baking powder
- 2 ml (½ t) salt
- 2 extra-large eggs, whisked
- 500 ml (2 c) water
- 250 ml (1 c) milk
- 50 ml (⅕ c) oil
- 15 ml (1 T) vinegar
- oil for frying

MUSHROOM FILLING
- 1 onion, finely chopped
- 250 g button mushrooms, sliced
- butter
- 5 ml (1 t) mixed dried herbs
- salt and freshly ground black pepper
- 15 ml (1 T) whole-wheat flour
- 80 ml (⅓ c) milk

APPLE FILLING
- 4 cooking apples, cored, peeled and diced
- 50 ml (⅕ c) raisins
- 5 ml (1 t) mixed spice
- 15 ml (1 T) honey
- 50 ml (⅕ c) water
- 50 ml (⅕ c) plain yoghurt

■ PANCAKES: Sift the whole-wheat flour, baking powder and salt in a mixing bowl. Add the bran left behind in the sieve to the bowl. Mix the remaining ingredients and add to the flour mixture, mixing well. Leave for 1 hour.

Pour a little oil into a pan and heat well. Remove any excess oil with paper towelling. Pour just enough pancake batter into the pan to cover the base. (Stir the batter each time before pouring it into the pan.) Bake until done on both sides and serve with a filling of your choice.

Makes about 16 pancakes.

■ MUSHROOM FILLING: Sauté the onion and mushrooms in a little butter until the onions are tender and translucent. Add the mixed herbs and season with salt and black pepper to taste.

Combine the whole-wheat flour and milk. Add to the mushroom mixture and simmer while stirring continuously until the mixture thickens. Fill the pancakes with the mixture and serve hot.

Enough for 4 pancakes.

■ APPLE FILLING: Heat the apples, raisins, mixed spice, honey and water in a saucepan. Simmer until the apples are tender but still firm and most of the liquid has evaporated. Remove from the heat and mix with the yoghurt. Fill the pancakes and serve hot.

Enough for 5 pancakes.

Fritters

Mealie-meal porridge fritters with cheese

Ernalene Digue of Blackhill uses leftover porridge to make delicious fritters. Add Cheddar cheese and mustard for extra tang.

- 250 ml (1 c) slack mealie-meal porridge
- 250 ml (1 c) cake flour
- 5 ml (1 t) salt
- 2 ml (½ t) mustard powder
- 2 ml (½ t) cayenne pepper
- 15 ml (1 T) baking powder
- 250 ml (1 c) grated Cheddar cheese
- 1 extra-large egg, whisked
- little milk (optional)
- oil for deep frying
- braai spice and finely chopped parsley for sprinkling on top

Mix the porridge, cake flour, salt, mustard powder, cayenne pepper, baking powder and cheese in a mixing bowl. Add the whisked egg and a little milk if the dough is too stiff.

Heat sufficient oil in a heavy-bottomed saucepan. Drop spoonfuls of the batter into the hot oil. Fry until golden brown on the outside and drain on paper towelling. Sprinkle with braai spice and parsley while the fritters are still hot. (To make bite-sized fritters, drop the batter into the oil using a teaspoon.)

Serve hot.

Makes about 10 fairly large fritters.

Mealie-meal porridge fritters with cheese (back) and Mealie-meal porridge fritters with cinnamon sugar (p. 80)

Mealie-meal porridge fritters with cinnamon sugar

Another recipe from Ernalene Digue of Blackhill. Roll these fritters in cinnamon sugar for an in-between snack.

- 2 extra-large eggs
- 250 ml (1 c) slack mealie-meal porridge
- 450 ml (1⅘ c) cake flour
- 10 ml (2 t) baking powder
- pinch salt
- about 50 ml (⅕ c) milk
- oil for deep frying
- cinnamon sugar for sprinkling on top

Whisk the eggs in a mixing bowl and mix in the mealie-meal porridge. Add the cake flour, baking powder and salt. Mix well. Add the milk to form a fairly slack batter.

Heat sufficient oil in a heavy-bottomed saucepan. Drop spoonfuls of the batter into the hot oil. (To make bite-sized fritters, use a teaspoon.) Fry until golden brown on the outside. Drain on paper towelling. Sprinkle the fritters with cinnamon sugar while still hot.

Serve hot.

Makes about 10 fairly large fritters.

Apple fritters

Because fruit is so inexpensive in Pietersburg, Mrs Gerda van der Berg writes she uses it in all kinds of ways, including to make these fritters.

- 500 ml (2 c) cake flour
- 5 ml (1 t) salt
- 250 ml (1 c) milk
- 2 extra-large eggs
- 250 ml (1 c) grated apple
- 125 ml (½ c) grated Cheddar cheese
- oil for deep frying
- cinnamon sugar

Mix the cake flour and salt in a large mixing bowl. Beat the milk and eggs together and add to the cake flour. Stir until smooth, add the apple and cheese and mix.

Heat oil in a pan and drop spoonfuls of the batter into the pan. Fry until brown on the outside and cooked inside. Roll in cinnamon sugar and serve luke-warm.

Makes about 19 fritters.

Apple fritters

Sandwich fritters

Sandwich fritters

Mrs Flo Lishman of Bluff, Durban, writes that these fritters are quick to make and are very filling.

- 375 ml (1½ c) cake flour
- pinch salt
- 12 ml (2½ t) baking powder
- 1 extra-large egg, whisked
- about 200 ml (⅘ c) water (enough to form a stiff batter)
- 6 slices white bread, crusts removed
- smooth strawberry jam
- oil for deep frying

Combine the cake flour, salt and baking powder and add the egg and water. Mix until smooth.

Spread three slices of bread with a thick layer of strawberry jam. Sandwich in twos with the remaining slices. Quarter each sandwich to make 12 triangles. Dip each triangle in the batter and deep-fry until golden brown. Drain on paper towelling. Serve hot or cold with custard if preferred.

Makes 12 triangles.

Oats fritters

Her mother used to make these fritters with leftover oats porridge when she was still a child, writes Mrs S. Crause of Knysna. They used to have them as a bed-time snack.

- 250 ml (1 c) cooked oats porridge
- 125 ml (½ c) cake flour
- 5 ml (1 t) baking powder
- pinch salt
- 1 extra-large egg, whisked
- oil for shallow frying

Mix all the ingredients except the oil and fry spoonfuls in heated oil until browned and cooked inside.

Serve hot with cinnamon sugar.

Makes 9 fritters.

Oats fritters

Super sandwiches

Whether it is open, closed or toasted, hardly a day goes by that we don't have a sandwich. Here are some delicious ideas for wholesome yet different sandwich fillings and toppings. Just right for a light meal, the picnic basket or lunch box.

Open sandwiches

Whole-wheat bread with Creole blackened chicken

At the Orchard Farmstall in Elgin, the wide selection of open sandwiches are always very popular as a light meal. Pierre Lombard, chef at the Orchard was given this recipe while on a trip to America. This sandwich is the *You* photographer's favourite.

BREAD
- 1 chicken breast fillet
- salt
- Creole spices (see recipe)
- 15 ml (1 T) oil
- 2 slices whole-wheat bread
- lettuce leaves, shredded
- mayonnaise
- few slices tomato

CREOLE SPICES
Mix:
- 5 ml (1 t) cayenne pepper
- 5 ml (1 t) white pepper
- 5 ml (1 t) black pepper
- 5 ml (1 t) dried thyme
- 5 ml (1 t) dried origanum
- 5 ml (1 t) brown sugar
- 15 ml (1 T) paprika
- 15 ml (1 T) crushed garlic

Place the chicken fillet between two layers of plastic wrap and flatten with the palm of your hand or with a meat mallet until about 2 mm thick. Season lightly with salt and spice generously on both sides with the spice mixture.

Whole-wheat bread with Creole blackened chicken

Heat a pan until very hot, add the oil and heat until smoking. Grill the chicken fillet for about 1 minute on each side until charred.

Meanwhile, place two slices of bread on a plate. Moisten the lettuce with mayonnaise, place on top of the bread and top with a few tomato slices. Place the chicken fillet on top of the slices and serve immediately.

Serves 1.

Camembert and bacon bruschetta

You can't improve on the combination of flavours for this open sandwich. Another recipe from the Orchard Farmstall.

GARLIC BUTTER
- 30 ml (2 T) butter
- 10 ml (2 t) crushed garlic
- 10 ml (2 t) freshly chopped parsley
- 30 ml (2 T) olive oil
- salt to taste

BREAD
- 2 slices bruschetta or French loaf, sliced diagonally
- few lettuce leaves
- 75 g mature Camembert cheese, sliced
- 3 rashers bacon, grilled
- 30 ml (2 T) apple jelly

- GARLIC BUTTER: Blend all the ingredients for the butter.
- BREAD: Butter the bread on both sides with the garlic butter. Arrange on a baking sheet and grill under the oven grill until lightly browned.

Transfer the bread to a plate, top with a few lettuce leaves and arrange the cheese and bacon on top. Serve immediately with the apple jelly.

Serves 1.

Health sandwich

A glass of freshly squeezed orange juice goes down well with this health sandwich, one of the favourite light meal selections at the Orchard Farmstall in Elgin.

- handful sunflower seeds
- oil
- 5 ml (1 t) soy sauce
- 2 slices whole-wheat bread
- few lettuce leaves
- few thin slices cucumber and tomato
- scoop of crumbly cottage cheese
- few orange segments
- paper-thin sliced apple
- few bean sprouts

Fry the sunflower seeds in a little oil until lightly browned.

Add the soy sauce and heat until most of the soy sauce has evaporated.

Place the whole-wheat bread on a plate and arrange all the ingredients on top. Sprinkle with the sunflower seeds.

Serves 1.

Tuna sandwich

Mrs Collins adds thinly sliced banana to the tuna mixture, but the sandwiches are just as good without.

- 1 can (185 g) tuna in brine, drained
- ½ onion, chopped and sautéed
- 30 ml (2 T) mayonnaise
- 15 ml (1 T) tomato sauce
- 15 ml (1 T) chutney
- few lettuce leaves
- 2 slices bread or 2 hotdog rolls
- 4 small gherkins, cut into fans (optional)

Flake the tuna and mix with the onion, mayonnaise, tomato sauce and chutney.

Place a few lettuce leaves on each slice of bread or in the rolls which have been sliced open halfway. Spoon the mixture on top. Garnish with gherkins, if preferred.

Serves 2.

- **Variations**
- **Winter variation:** Add 250 ml (1 c) grated Cheddar cheese to the mixture and spoon on top of the slices of bread. Toast under the oven grill until the cheese has melted.
- **Kids' variation:** Hollow out the hotdogs from one end only and fill with the filling.

Sandwiches and ideas for fillings and spreads

Basic egg spread

Sandwiches are easy to make, but often one runs out of ideas for what to put on them. If you have a bottle of this basic egg spread in the fridge you can vary it with any one of our suggestions. Serve with a piece of fruit, and you have a fully balanced meal.

- 12 hard-boiled eggs, finely chopped
- 200 ml (⅘ c) mayonnaise
- 3 ml (generous ½ t) salt
- pinch of pepper

Mix the eggs and mayonnaise together and season with salt and pepper to taste. Spoon into clean jars, close and store in the fridge until needed.

The mixture makes 700 ml and can be stored in the fridge for about a week. 100 ml (⅖ c) basic egg spread is enough for 4-6 sandwiches.

- **Variations**

Add any of the following to 100 ml of the basic egg spread and mix:

- 50 ml (⅕ c) grated Cheddar cheese and 15 ml (1 T) freshly chopped parsley
- 5 ml (1 t) curry powder and 5 ml (1 t) chutney
- 3 gherkins, finely chopped
- 30 ml (2 T) finely chopped and crisply fried bacon
- 30 ml (2 T) flaked tuna and 10 ml (2 t) tomato sauce
- 30 ml (2 T) savoury cottage cheese
- 15 ml (1 T) tomato sauce
- 5 ml (1 t) Worcester sauce
- 5 ml (1 t) prepared mustard
- 1 smoked sausage, finely chopped
- 30 ml (2 T) finely chopped ham or tongue
- 30 ml (2 T) finely chopped cooked chicken
- 30 ml (2 T) mashed pilchards and 10 ml (2 t) tomato sauce

Sandwich spread

She was given this recipe by her friend Carina van Zyl, writes Mrs Marian Leibbrandt of Jan Kempdorp. She says it lasts for weeks in the fridge.

- 1 English cucumber, grated or finely chopped
- 1 onion, finely chopped
- 2-4 carrots, finely grated
- 1-2 green peppers, finely chopped
- 1-2 red peppers, finely chopped
- 750 ml (3 c) white grape vinegar
- about 500 ml (2 c) mayonnaise

Mix all the vegetables in a mixing bowl. Pour over the vinegar and leave for 24 hours.

Drain well, press out all the liquid and mix with just enough mayonnaise to make a spread. (Reserve the vinegar for salad dressing.) Spoon the sandwich spread into clean jars, close and store in the fridge until it is needed.

Makes about 800 ml spread. 100 ml is enough for 4-6 sandwiches.

Home-made cheese spread

She was given the recipe for this economical cheese spread by a friend, writes Joan O'Neill of Warrenton.

- 500-750 ml (2-3 c) milk
- 1 kg processed cheese, grated
- 500 g margarine
- seasoning (such as Aromat)
- 500 ml (2 c) finely grated biltong (optional)

Heat the milk, add the cheese and melt slowly over low heat while stirring continuously.

Stir in the margarine and season to taste with Aromat. Add the biltong if preferred and mix. Spoon into clean, sterilised bottles while still hot. Store in the fridge.

Makes 1,5 litres.

Basic egg spread with variations

Egg and onion spread

Mrs I. Smuts of Durbanville makes this delicious sandwich spread herself. You don't need to butter the sandwiches when using this spread.

- 8 hard-boiled eggs, finely chopped
- 2 medium onions, grated
- 37,5 ml (2½ T) mayonnaise
- 100 g (250 ml) Cheddar cheese, grated
- 5 ml (1 t) lemon juice
- 2 ml (½ t) black pepper
- 5 ml (1 t) salt
- 20 ml (4 t) finely chopped fresh parsley

Combine the eggs, onions, mayonnaise and Cheddar cheese in a mixing bowl. Add the lemon juice and seasonings and mix well. Spoon into clean jars, close and store in the fridge until needed.
Makes about 500 ml.

Ham and cottage cheese spread

A wonderful spread to go with your favourite bread.

- 100 g (150 ml) ham, finely chopped
- 150 ml (⅗ c) smooth cottage cheese
- 4 ml (¾ t) mustard powder
- 60 ml (¼ c) grated Cheddar cheese

Combine the ham and cottage cheese in a mixing bowl. Season with mustard powder and mix well. Store in the fridge until needed. Spread on a slice of whole-wheat bread and sprinkle with a little grated Cheddar cheese. Cover with a buttered slice of whole-wheat bread.
Enough for 2 sandwiches.

Tuna and vegetable filling

Mrs Peggy Beukes of Firgrove also serves this tuna and vegetable mixture as a starter or main course for a light summer meal.

TUNA MIXTURE
- 2 tins (200 g each) tuna in brine, drained
- 1 apple, peeled and cubed
- 2 tomatoes, chopped
- 1 onion, chopped
- ½ green pepper, seeded and chopped
- 1 potato, boiled and cubed

DRESSING
- 125 ml (½ c) mayonnaise
- 125 ml (½ c) fresh cream
- 25 ml (5 t) lemon juice
- 2 ml (½ t) paprika
- salt and freshly ground black pepper

- TUNA MIXTURE: Flake the tuna in a mixing bowl and add the remaining ingredients. Mix.
- DRESSING: Mix the mayonnaise, cream, lemon juice and paprika. Season to taste with salt and pepper and add to the fish mixture. Mix well and chill for 30 minutes. The mixture keeps well in the fridge for up to two days.
Makes about 300 ml filling.

More ideas for sandwiches

Cheese fillings: Grated cheese and cottage or cream cheese are the ideal base for numerous imaginative mixed spreads:

- Mix grated cheese with tomato sauce, Worcester sauce and a little butter.
- Mix cream or cottage cheese with:
  - a chopped onion, parsley and cucumber;
  - fried bacon;
  - shredded cooked meat;
  - peanut butter or fish paste;
  - honey and nuts;
  - grated Cheddar cheese and finely chopped onion.

Fruit fillings: Combine dried and fresh fruit with a variety of ingredients from the grocery cupboard and fridge to create deliciously exotic spreads:

- Mix sultanas and peanut butter.
- Mince dates and raisins or sultanas and mix with chopped nuts and butter.
- Butter a slice of bread and cover with banana slices. Sprinkle a little coconut on top.
- Mix cottage cheese with stewed prunes or raisins.
- Mix chopped dates with honey and lemon juice.

Coleslaw sandwich

Substitute some of the filling ingredients with leftover coleslaw. This recipe was also sent in by Mrs Moore.

- 2 cabbage leaves, finely shredded
- 1 large carrot, scraped clean and cut into strips
- 4 mushrooms, sliced (optional)
- 1 tomato, sliced
- 4-6 slices whole-wheat bread
- 50 ml (⅕ c) raisins
- 50 ml (⅕ c) bean sprouts (optional)
- 50 ml (⅕ c) plain yoghurt

Arrange all the vegetables on two to three slices bread. Sprinkle the raisins and bean sprouts on top and spoon the yoghurt on top.

Cover with the remaining two to three slices bread and halve the sandwiches. Wrap in wax paper and store in the fridge.

Serves 2-3.

Coleslaw sandwich

Potato salad rolls

Use leftover potato salad as a filling for bread rolls. Mrs J.D. Moore of Goodwood adds slices of cold meat to the rolls.

- 3-4 lettuce leaves
- 2 slices ham, halved
- 2 slices salami, halved
- 3-4 rolls, sliced open and buttered
- 200 g leftover potato salad
- 2 chives, chopped
- salt and cayenne pepper

Arrange the lettuce leaves, and ham and salami slices inside the rolls. Top with potato salad and sprinkle with chives. Season with salt and cayenne pepper if preferred and wrap in wax paper.
Serves 2-3.

Snackwich pies

Prepare this pastry and bake pies in a Snackwich. The recipes for the pastry and two fillings were sent in by Mrs Emily Mundell of Bellville in the Cape. The dough must be made with butter as margarine or oil will leave a sticky film on the pastry, writes Mrs Mundell.

SHORT-CRUST PASTRY
- 500 ml (2 c) cake flour
- pinch salt
- 10 ml (2 t) baking powder
- 250 ml (1 c) soft butter (not margarine)
- 2 extra-large eggs, whisked
- 1 egg white

BANANA AND BULLY BEEF FILLING
- 1 can (300 g) bully beef, mashed or diced
- 6 rashers bacon, fried and finely chopped (optional)
- 2 bananas, mashed
- 30 ml (2 T) mayonnaise
- salt and pepper to taste

CHICKEN AND CHEESE FILLING
- 200 g cooked chicken, shredded
- 1 onion, finely chopped
- 100 g Tusser's cheese, grated
- 2 egg yolks, whisked

■ SHORT-CRUST PASTRY: Sift together the cake flour, salt and baking powder. Rub in the butter with your fingertips until the mixture resembles breadcrumbs. Add the eggs and mix to form a stiff dough.

Chill until needed. Roll out the dough until 3 mm thick and cut into 10 x 12-cm pieces. Spoon a little of the filling on half the pastry pieces, lightly brush the sides with whisked egg white and cover with the other pastry pieces.

Place two pies in the Snackwich and toast until golden brown on the outside and done or prepare in a jaffle pan.

Enough dough for 5 whole pies (or jaffles) or 10 triangles.
■ BANANA AND BULLY BEEF FILLING: Mix all the ingredients and use as a filling for the pies or on bread.

Enough for 6 whole pies (or jaffles or toasted sandwiches), or 12 triangles.
■ CHICKEN AND CHEESE FILLING: Mix all the ingredients and use as a filling for the pies or on bread.

Enough for 6 whole pies (or jaffles or toasted sandwiches), or 12 triangles.

Toasted sandwiches

De luxe cheese toasties

Toasted sandwiches are always a firm favourite for a light supper. Store this mixture in the fridge for up to three days and use as a sandwich filling, writes Mrs S. Chetty of Marlboro.

- 125 ml (½ c) stuffed green olives, chopped
- 250 ml (1 c) grated Cheddar cheese
- 4 spring onions, chopped
- 5 ml (1 t) curry powder
- 25 ml (5 t) tomato sauce
- 125 ml (½ c) mayonnaise
- 4-6 slices white or brown bread
- butter

Mix all the ingredients together, except the bread and butter. Toast the bread on one side only and butter on the untoasted side only. Spoon a little of the mixture onto each slice of bread and grill until brown on top.
Makes 4-6 toasties.

Boerewors toasties

The recipe comes in handy when you're on holiday and there's sausage left over after a braai, writes Mrs I.A. du Plessis of Parow.

- 6 slices bread
- butter
- 1 onion, finely chopped
- oil
- 2 tomatoes, skinned and finely chopped
- 30 ml (2 T) mayonnaise
- 5 ml (1 t) mustard powder
- 300 g cooked boerewors
- 30 ml (2 T) finely chopped parsley
- 125 ml (½ c) grated Cheddar cheese

Switch on the oven grill.

Lightly butter the bread and place on a baking sheet, buttered side up.

Sauté the onion in a little oil until tender. Add the tomatoes and simmer for 5 minutes. Add the mayonnaise and mustard powder.

Cut the boerewors into pieces and add. Simmer for another 5 minutes. Spoon on top of the bread slices, sprinkle with the parsley and cheese and grill for 5-10 minutes or until the cheese has melted.

Serve hot.

Serves 4.

Boerewors toasties

Toasted ham sandwiches

Sandwiches prepared the night before and then toasted the following morning make a delicious lunch-time snack.

- 110 g butter or margarine
- 5-12,5 ml (1-2½ t) mustard powder
- 10 slices bread
- 5 slices ham
- 3 eggs, whisked
- 60 ml (¼ c) milk
- oil

Mix the butter and mustard powder and spread the bread slices with the mixture.

Place a slice of ham on five of the bread slices and cover with the remaining slices. Secure with tooth-picks.

Beat the eggs and milk and dip each sandwich in the egg mixture.

Heat the oil in a pan and fry each sandwich until browned on both sides.

Makes 5 sandwiches.

Spinach and cheese toasties

After a big Sunday lunch they usually just have sand-wiches for supper, writes Mrs Picey Collins of La Rochelle. Her family often enjoy the sandwiches more than lunch because they always experiment with new fillings.

- 2 rashers bacon
- 1 onion, chopped
- 1 clove garlic, crushed
- oil
- 6-8 spinach leaves (stalks removed), shredded
- 2 hard-boiled eggs, mashed
- 200 ml (⅘ c) grated Cheddar cheese
- 250 ml (1 c) mayonnaise
- 1 egg, whisked
- dash lemon juice
- salt and freshly black pepper to taste
- 4-6 slices rye bread
- few thin strips red pepper (optional)

Switch on the oven grill.

Fry the bacon until done and slightly crisp. Remove from the pan and chop finely.

Sauté the onion and garlic in a little oil in the same pan until tender. Add the spinach leaves and sauté until soft.

Mix the spinach mixture with the bacon, eggs, cheese, mayonnaise and whisked egg and season with lemon juice, salt and pepper.

Place the slices of rye bread on a baking sheet and spoon the spinach mixture on top. Garnish with strips of red pepper if preferred. Grill until golden brown on top.

Serves 4-6.

Garlic and cheese toasties

Elmarie Esterhuizen of Krugersdorp often surprises her guests with these tasty snacks when they have a braai.

- 500 ml (2 c) grated Cheddar cheese
- 5 ml (1 t) crushed garlic
- 125 ml (½ c) mayonnaise
- 1 short French loaf, cut into 1-cm-thick slices

Switch on the oven grill.

Mix the grated cheese, garlic and mayonnaise and spread each slice of bread with about a teaspoonful of the mixture. Arrange the bread slices on a baking sheet and grill for about 2 minutes or until the cheese has melted and is golden brown.

Makes 18 toasties.

Toast with anchovies and tomato

A delicious, quick 'n easy snack, says Mrs Beverley Smit of Penhill.

- 6-8 slices brown or rye bread, lightly toasted
- 500 ml (2 c) grated Cheddar cheese
- 1 large clove garlic, crushed
- 1 large tomato, sliced
- 1 tin (50 g) anchovy fillets, drained

Switch on the oven grill.

Arrange the toast on a baking sheet. Divide the cheese evenly between the slices of toast. Sprinkle with garlic and place a slice of tomato on each slice of toast. Arrange the anchovy fillets on top and grill for a few minutes or until the cheese has melted.

Serve immediately.

Serves 4-6.

Toast with anchovies and tomato

French loaf toasties

Mrs I.A. du Plessis of Parow makes these delicious toasties topped with sardines and mozzarella cheese.

- 1 short French loaf, cut into 1-cm-thick slices (about 22 slices)
- olive oil
- 1 onion, finely chopped
- 2 cloves garlic, crushed
- 2 cans (102 g each) sardines, mashed
- 15 ml (1 T) freshly chopped parsley
- salt and freshly ground black pepper
- 150 g mozzarella cheese, sliced

Switch on the oven grill. Spray a baking sheet with nonstick spray or grease well with butter or margarine.

Arrange the slices of bread on the baking sheet and grill on one side until brown. Turn over and brush the other side with olive oil. Set aside.

Sauté the onion and garlic in a little oil until soft. Remove from the pan and mix with the sardines and parsley. Season with salt and pepper and spoon on top of the bread slices. Top each slice of bread with a slice of cheese and grill until the cheese has melted.

Serve immediately.

Makes about 22 slices.

Window bread

A nice alternative for breakfast.

- few slices white or brown bread
- melted butter
- 1 egg per slice of bread
- salt and freshly ground black pepper
- chopped fresh parsley

Using a biscuit cutter, cut out a circle in the centre of each slice of bread. Fry the bread in melted butter until brown on both sides.

Place one or two slices of bread in the pan and break an egg into each hollow. Fry until the eggs have set. Season the eggs to taste with salt and black pepper. Sprinkle with chopped parsley and serve immediately.

Jaffles

Make a large batch of jaffles at a time and freeze them for up to one month. If you do not have a jaffle pan, use a Snackwich instead. Add a little curry to the mince if preferred.

- few slices brown or white bread
- butter
- cooked savoury mince with plenty of vegetables added

FOR 1 JAFFLE: Butter two slices of bread well on both sides. Spoon a generous helping of the mince mixture on top of one slice of bread and cover with the other slice.

Butter the inside of the jaffle pan and place the sandwich inside. Close the jaffle pan and place it on top of a heated stove plate or gas stove. Heat until the bread has browned on both sides.

Saturday lunch rolls

Carmin Harty of Parkhurst writes that she refuses to make a dish if it takes longer than 30 minutes to prepare. She likes to serve these stuffed rolls for a quick Saturday lunch.

- 8-10 round rolls
- oil
- 1 onion, chopped
- 1 clove garlic, crushed
- 1 tomato, skinned and chopped
- 1 can (410 g) mushroom soup
- 250 ml (1 c) cream
- salt and freshly ground black pepper
- pinch sugar
- grated cheese for sprinkling on top

Preheat the oven to 180 °C (350 °F).

Cut off the tops of the rolls and hollow the rolls out, leaving a 1-cm edge all the way around. Reserve the leftover pieces of bread.

Brush the tops and inside of the rolls with oil and place on a baking sheet. Heat in the oven until the rolls are crisp.

Sauté the onion and garlic in a little oil until tender. Add the tomato and simmer until a purée is formed. Add mushroom soup, cream and pieces of bread and simmer until the mixture is nice and thick. Season to taste with salt and pepper and sugar.

Spoon the mixture into the hollowed-out rolls, sprinkle with cheese and grill until the cheese has just melted. Replace the tops and serve immediately.

Serves 8.

Saturday lunch rolls

Brinjal and mozzarella on toast

Speciality shops and bakeries now stock a wonderful selection of flavoured breads. Use the bread of your choice to prepare this sandwich.

- 1 large brinjal
- 30 ml (2 T) olive oil
- 15 ml (1 T) lemon juice
- freshly ground black pepper
- 1 onion, cut into wedges
- 1 tomato, cut into thick slices
- 150 g mozzarella cheese, sliced
- 2 thick slices bread of your choice, lightly toasted (olive bread, cheese-and-onion bread, bread with sun-dried tomatoes or garlic bread)

Switch on the oven grill. Spray a baking sheet with nonstick spray or grease well with butter or margarine. Slice the brinjal into 1-cm-thick slices lengthwise.

Blend the olive oil and lemon juice and brush the brinjal slices with the mixture. Season with freshly ground black pepper.

Place brinjal slices on the baking sheet along with the onion and tomato and grill for about 6 minutes. Remove the tomato and onion, turn brinjal slices and grill on other side for about 6 minutes or until golden brown.

Place the slices of mozzarella cheese on top of the brinjal and grill until the cheese has melted.

Transfer the brinjal slices to the toasted bread and top with the onion and tomato.

Serve hot with a salad.

Serves 1-2.

Sardine surprise

Mrs Babsie Meintjies of Lindley uses this recipe to make a filling for toasted Snackwich sandwiches or jaffles, to spread on toast or for a light savoury supper-time tart.

BREAD
- 12 slices bread
- butter

SARDINE FILLING
- 1 tin (105 g) sardines, drained
- 1 tomato, diced
- 1 small onion, finely chopped
- 250 ml (1 c) grated Cheddar cheese
- salt and pepper to taste

Butter the slices of bread on one side only.

- SARDINE FILLING: Lightly flake the sardines and mix with the remaining filling ingredients. Spoon the filling on top of six slices of bread and cover with the remaining six slices. Toast in a Snackwich until brown on both sides.

Makes 6 jaffles or sandwiches, or 12 triangles.

Picnic loaves

Picnic loaf

A recipe from Elsabé Robberts of Brackenhurst.

BREAD
- 1 small rye loaf
- garlic oil

FILLING
- 125 g creamed cottage cheese
- 50 g soft butter
- 2 hard-boiled eggs, finely chopped
- 6 mushrooms, sliced and fried
- 1 clove garlic, crushed
- 100 g ham, diced
- 1 gherkin, finely chopped
- 10 stuffed olives, halved
- salt and freshly ground black pepper
- 7 ml (1½ t) gelatine
- 20 ml (4 t) cold water

Preheat the oven to 200 °C (400 °F).

Remove the crust and hollow out the rye loaf, leaving a 1-cm-thick edge all the way around. (Use the left-over pieces of bread to make breadcrumbs and freeze.)

Brush the inside of the hollowed-out loaf and crust with a little garlic oil. Place on a baking sheet and grill for a few minutes until crisp.

- FILLING: Blend the cottage cheese and butter. Add the remaining filling ingredients, except the gelatine and water, and mix lightly.

Sprinkle the gelatine over the cold water and leave for a few minutes until spongy. Heat for about 40 seconds on 100 per cent power in the microwave oven until melted, but do not bring to the boil. Stir well.

Add the gelatine to the filling mixture, mix and spoon into the prepared loaf. Replace the crust and chill until the filling has set. Cut into slices or wedges before serving.

Makes a medium loaf.

Picnic loaf

Seed chicken in a loaf

If you're going on a picnic, simply wrap the loaf in aluminium foil and newspaper to keep it beautifully warm, writes Elna Mattheus of Pretoria.

CHICKEN
- 125 ml (½ c) cake flour
- 25 ml (5 t) sesame seeds
- 2 ml (½ t) dried basil
- 5 ml (1 t) dried tarragon
- 7 ml (1½ t) poppy seeds
- 5 ml (1 t) salt
- black pepper to taste
- 2 egg whites, lightly whisked
- 6 chicken thighs

BREAD
- 1 large round loaf, such as a Portuguese loaf
- 80 ml (⅓ c) melted butter
- 45 ml (3 T) sesame seeds
- 15 ml (1 T) poppy seeds
- 5 ml (1 t) dried basil
- 5 ml (1 t) dried tarragon

DRESSING
- ¼ English cucumber, diced
- 1 clove garlic, crushed
- 125 ml (½ c) plain yoghurt
- salt and black pepper to taste
- chopped parsley (optional)

Preheat the oven to 180 °C (350 °F).

■ CHICKEN: Combine all the ingredients for the chicken, except the egg whites and chicken thighs. Dip the chicken thighs into the egg white and roll them in the cake flour mixture. Arrange the chicken pieces on the rack of an oven roasting tin. Cover with aluminium foil and bake in the oven for about 1 hour or until the chicken is done. Remove the aluminium foil just before the end of the cooking time to allow the chicken to brown lightly.

■ BREAD: Cut off the top of the loaf of bread and reserve it as a lid. Hollow out the bread, leaving an edge of about 1,5 cm thick all the way around. (Use the leftover pieces of bread to make breadcrumbs and freeze.)

Mix the melted butter with the sesame and poppy seeds and seasonings. Brush the inside of the loaf and bottom of the bread crust with the mixture. Place the loaf and lid on a baking sheet and toast lightly in the oven.

■ DRESSING: Blend all the ingredients for the dressing and pour it into small serving bowls.

Place all the chicken pieces inside the loaf and cover with the lid. Decorate with sprigs of parsley if preferred.

Guests can help themselves to the chicken and a slice of bread. Serve with the cucumber dressing.
Serves 4-6.

Round picnic loaf

- 1 round or oval loaf
- butter
- 6 slices ham, diced
- 2 extra-large hard-boiled eggs, sliced
- about ¼ cucumber, sliced and quartered
- 1 small yellow pepper, diced
- 1 small onion, finely chopped
- 6-8 black or green olives, halved
- 25 ml (5 t) olive oil
- 25 ml (5 t) balsamic vinegar

Slice off the top of the round loaf, and hollow out and butter the inside of the loaf. (Use the leftover pieces of bread to make breadcrumbs and freeze.) Mix the ham, eggs, cucumber, pepper, onion and olives in a mixing bowl.

Blend the olive oil and balsamic vinegar. Sprinkle over the ham mixture. Spoon the filling into the hollowed-out loaf.

Return the lid and secure with a piece of string if preferred.
Serves 4.

Pita bread with salami

A delightful bread for the picnic basket. Lightly butter the pitas on the inside to prevent them from becoming soggy.

- 4-6 lettuce leaves, rinsed and patted dry
- 4-6 pita breads, halved
- 8 slices salami, quartered
- 60 ml (¼ c) sour cream
- 60 ml (¼ c) mayonnaise
- 5 ml (1 t) prepared mustard

Place the lettuce leaves in the hollow of each pita bread. Mix the remaining ingredients together and spoon into the pita bread.
Serves 4-6.

■ Variation

Shred the lettuce leaves and slice the salami. Mix with the dressing before spooning into the pita bread. The mixture also makes a delicious topping or filling for open or closed sandwiches.

Seed chicken in a loaf

Italian picnic loaf

Italian salad dressing adds the finishing touch to this beautiful picnic loaf.

- 1 large round Italian loaf
- 30 ml (2 T) Italian salad dressing
- 2 medium tomatoes, sliced
- 1 small head lettuce, well rinsed and shredded
- 200 g strong cheese, thinly sliced
- 250 g French polony, thinly sliced

Cut a thick, round slice off the top of the bread and hollow out the loaf, leaving an edge about 1,5 cm thick all around. (Use the leftover pieces of bread to make breadcrumbs and freeze.) Brush the inside of the loaf with the salad dressing.

Arrange layers of tomato, shredded lettuce, cheese and polony inside the loaf, pressing the ingredients firmly into the hollow. Sprinkle with the remaining salad dressing. Cover the loaf with the sliced-off crust and secure with a piece of string. Wrap the bread in aluminium foil and chill.

Slice just before serving.

Serves 4-6.

Baked bread and cheese (1)

Cube the leftover bread from the hollowed-out loaf and toast lightly. Serve with the stuffed loaf for dipping into the cheese mixture. Alternatively, serve the loaf with a variety of vegetable crudités. It's excellent served with drinks or for taking along on a picnic.

1 round loaf such as a Portuguese loaf

FILLING
- 250 ml (1 c) mozzarella or Tusser's cheese, grated
- 180 ml (¾ c) cream cheese
- 60 ml (¼ c) grated Parmesan cheese
- 1 small green pepper, seeded and diced
- 1 small red pepper, seeded and diced
- 1 clove garlic, crushed
- 5 ml (1 t) ground cumin (jeera)
- salt and black pepper to taste

Preheat the oven to 200 °C (400 °F).

Cut off the top of the loaf of bread and hollow it out, leaving an edge about 1,5 cm thick all the way around. (Reserve the crust as a lid.) Cube the leftover pieces of bread and arrange on a baking sheet.

■ FILLING: Mix all the ingredients for the filling and spoon into the prepared loaf. Cover with the crust and wrap in aluminium foil. Place the loaf on a baking sheet and bake in the oven for 1 hour.

Place the baking sheet with the bread cubes in the oven and toast for about 10 minutes until golden brown.

Carefully remove the aluminium foil and remove the crust. Stir the cheese mixture until creamy. Serve the cheese-filled bread with the toasted bread cubes. Once the filling is less, guests can help themselves to a slice of bread.

Serves 6-8.

Baked bread and cheese (2)

This cheese filling is flavoured with bacon, onions and green pepper. It's perfect party fare or for eating outdoors on a picnic.

- 500 g bacon, chopped
- 1 round or oval loaf
- 250 g Tusser's cheese
- 250 ml (1 c) sour cream
- 125 ml (½ c) chopped green pepper (optional)
- 125 ml (½ c) thinly sliced onion

Preheat the oven to 180 °C (350 °F).

Fry the bacon over medium heat until crisp. Remove from the pan with a slotted spoon and set aside. Reserve 45 ml of the bacon fat and pour off the rest.

Cut off the top of the bread and hollow it out: Remove the soft inside part, leaving an edge and base about 2 cm thick. Cut the leftover bread into fingers about 5 cm long and 1 cm thick. (Reserve the top for a lid.)

Brush the inside of the hollowed-out loaf as well as the top with the bacon fat. Place the loaf on a baking sheet and arrange the bread fingers in a single layer around it. Bake for about 15 minutes until just crisp.

Meanwhile, grate the Tusser's cheese finely or chop it finely in a food processor. Add the sour cream, mixing until a smooth paste is formed. Stir in the bacon, green pepper and onion.

Remove the crisped loaf from the oven and pour the cheese mixture into the hollow. Bake for another 20 minutes. Transfer the loaf to a serving platter and arrange the toasted bread fingers around it.

Dip the bread fingers into the cheese filling. Once the cheese filling is finished, cut the bread into pieces and serve.

Makes 1 medium loaf.

■ Variation

If preferred, gently sauté the green pepper and onion in oil before mixing it with the cheese.

Stuffed French loaf

Stuffed French loaf

Melinda Harrison of Vereeniging sent us a few delicious recipes, including this one for a stuffed French loaf.

- 1 small French loaf
- 30 ml (2 T) olive oil
- little anchovy paste
- 1-2 tomatoes, sliced
- 1 green pepper, seeded and diced
- 90 g black olives, stoned and halved
- 60 g capers

Halve the French loaf lengthwise and hollow out slightly. (Use the leftover bread to make breadcrumbs and freeze.)

Brush the inside of the loaf with olive oil and spread with a little anchovy paste. Arrange the tomato slices in the bottom of the loaf.

Mix the remaining ingredients and spoon on top of the tomato slices. Cover with the top half of the loaf and serve.

Serves 4-6.

From the microwave oven

Use the microwave oven for baking anything from banana loaves to mealie bread, and even griddlecakes, scones and rusks. It's also easy to make jam in the microwave oven. Serve with oven-fresh bread and lashings of butter.

Bread, griddlecakes, scones and rusks

Easy microwaved date loaf

Louise Laubscher of Somerset West sent us three excellent recipes for microwaved loaf cakes.

- 250 g stoned dates, finely chopped
- 50 g butter
- 200 ml (⅘ c) soft brown sugar
- 200 ml (⅘ c) water
- 5 ml (1 t) bicarbonate of soda
- 1 extra-large egg, whisked
- 375 ml (1½ c) self-raising flour
- 5 ml (1 t) salt
- ½ packet (50 g) diced almonds
- sugar (optional)

Spray a 25 x 12 x 8-cm microwave-proof loaf tin with nonstick spray. Line the bottom of the tin with paper towelling.

Mix the dates, butter, sugar and water in a large microwave-proof bowl and microwave for 5 minutes on 70 per cent power (medium high). Stir after 3 minutes. Add the bicarbonate of soda and cool for about 2 minutes.

Add the egg and mix. Sift the self-raising flour and salt together and add to the mixture along with the almonds. Mix lightly until just blended. Turn into the prepared tin and place in the microwave oven on an upturned saucer. Microwave for 8-9 minutes on 70 per cent power (medium high) or until done. Leave in the tin for about 5 minutes, then turn out onto a wire rack to cool. Remove the paper towelling and sprinkle with a little sugar if preferred. Slice and serve with butter.

Makes 1 medium loaf.

Recipe tested in a 600-watt oven.

From bottom left, clockwise: Easy microwaved banana loaf, Easy microwaved date loaf and Easy microwaved spiced apple loaf (p. 104)

Easy microwaved banana loaf

Another recipe sent in by Louisa Laubscher. The date and banana loaves freeze well.

- 125 g margarine
- 250 ml (1 c) soft brown sugar
- 2 extra-large eggs
- 4 ripe bananas, mashed
- 500 ml (2 c) cake flour
- 10 ml (2 t) baking powder
- 5 ml (1 t) bicarbonate of soda
- 80 ml (⅓ c) water
- ½ packet (50 g) diced almonds
- 5 ml (1 t) cinnamon
- sugar (optional)

Spray a 25 x 12 x 8-cm microwave-proof loaf tin with nonstick spray. Line the bottom of the pan with paper towelling.

Beat the margarine until light and creamy. Add small quantities of sugar at a time while beating continuously. Add the eggs one by one, beating well after each addition.

Add the mashed banana and mix.

Sift the cake flour and baking powder together. Dissolve the bicarbonate of soda in the water and add to the butter mixture, alternating with the flour mixture. Add the almonds and cinnamon and mix lightly. Turn the batter into the prepared loaf tin and place in the microwave oven on an upturned saucer. Microwave for 12-14 minutes on 70 per cent power (medium high) or until the loaf has shrunk slightly from the sides of the tin. Leave in the tin for about 5 minutes before turning out onto a wire rack to cool completely. Remove the paper towelling and sprinkle with a little sugar if preferred. Slice and serve with butter.

Makes 1 medium loaf.

Recipe tested in a 600-watt oven.

Easy microwaved spiced apple loaf

This loaf also freezes well, writes Louisa Laubsher.

- 375 ml (1½ c) cake flour
- 5 ml (1 t) salt
- 2 ml (½ t) cloves
- 5 ml (1 t) nutmeg
- 5 ml (1 t) bicarbonate of soda
- 250 ml (1 c) soft brown sugar
- 2 extra-large eggs, whisked
- 125 ml (½ c) oil
- 150 g dried fruitcake mix
- 1 can (385 g) pie apples, coarsely chopped
- sugar (optional)

Spray a 25 x 12 x 8-cm microwave-proof loaf tin with nonstick spray. Line the bottom of the pan with paper towelling.

Sift the cake flour, salt, spices and bicarbonate of soda together in a mixing bowl. Add sugar and mix. Add eggs and oil, beating well for about 2 minutes.

Add the fruitcake mix and pie apples and mix well. Turn the batter into the prepared tin and place in the microwave oven on an upturned saucer. Microwave for 12-14 minutes on 70 per cent power (medium high) or until the loaf shrinks slightly from the sides of the tin.

Leave in the tin for about 5 minutes before turning out onto a wire rack to cool. Remove the paper towelling and sprinkle a little sugar over the crust if preferred. Slice and serve.

Makes 1 medium loaf.

Tested in a 600-watt oven.

Easy microwaved mealie bread

A nourishing mealie bread that's quick and easy to make in the microwave oven.

- 2 extra-large eggs
- 125 ml (½ c) milk
- 1 can (410 g) cream-style sweetcorn
- 250 ml (1 c) whole-wheat flour
- 250 ml (1 c) mealie meal
- 15 ml (1 T) baking powder
- 5 ml (1 t) salt
- 60 ml (¼ c) sugar

Spray a 23 x 13-cm microwave-proof loaf tin with nonstick spray and line the bottom of the tin with paper towelling.

Whisk the eggs and milk together and add the sweetcorn.

Sift together the dry ingredients and add the bran left behind in the sieve to the bowl. Add the sugar.

Mix the egg mixture and dry ingredients lightly and turn the batter into the prepared tin. Place the tin on an upturned saucer and microwave for 12-14 minutes on 70 per cent power (medium high) or until the loaf shrinks from the sides of the tin. Cool slightly in the pan before turning out onto a wire rack. Remove the paper towelling and serve with butter.

Makes 1 medium loaf.

Tested in a 650-watt oven.

Easy microwaved scones

Miss L. Schoeman of Johannesburg varies her basic scone recipe so she can serve a selection of scones at tea time.

- 500 ml (2 c) self-raising flour
- pinch salt
- 60 g soft butter
- 60 ml (¼ c) caster sugar
- 1 extra-large egg, whisked
- 100 ml (⅖ c) milk
- bran

Sift together the self-raising flour and salt in a large mixing bowl. Rub in the butter with your fingertips until the mixture resembles breadcrumbs. Add the caster sugar.

Mix the egg and milk and add. Mix lightly with a spatula until just blended. On a floured surface, roll out the dough until it is 2 cm thick. Cut out circles 6 cm in diameter. Line the turntable of the microwave oven with a double layer of paper towelling and arrange a batch of 6 scones on it. Microwave for 1 minute on 100 per cent power (high). Turn the scones over and microwave for 1 minute more on 100 per cent power (high).

Serve warm with butter, cheese and jam.

Makes 6-8 scones.

Tested in a 600-watt oven.

Variations

■ **Whole-wheat scones:** Substitute 250 ml (1 c) whole-wheat flour for 250 ml (1 c) self-raising flour. Add 7 ml (1½ t) baking powder to the dry ingredients and proceed as described in the basic scone recipe, but sprinkle the scones with sesame seeds before microwaving.

■ **Raisin and nut scones:** Add 50 ml (⅕ c) raisins and 50 ml (⅕ c) chopped nuts to the dry ingredients. Proceed as described in the basic scone recipe, brushing the scones with melted honey before microwaving.

Easy microwaved scones with variations

Easy microwaved griddlecakes

Mrs Elna de Klerk of Oakdale, Bellville, microwaves her griddlecakes before browning them briefly over the coals or under a preheated oven grill. The griddlecakes can also be baked in the microwave until done and then frozen, so they're ready when you decide to have a braai.

- 500 g self-raising flour
- 10 ml (2 t) sugar
- 5 ml (1 t) salt
- 2 ml (½ t) aniseed
- 2 ml (½ t) caraway seed
- 1 ml (¼ t) nutmeg
- 45 ml (3 T) oil
- 1 can (340 ml) beer
- oil to brush with

Combine the self-raising flour, sugar and spices in a mixing bowl. Make a hollow in the centre of the flour mixture and pour in the oil. Slowly add and stir in the beer. Mix to form a soft, manageable dough, similar to a scone dough. Divide into 12 uniform pieces and shape into balls. Brush each one with oil, cover with plastic wrap and leave for 10 minutes.

Lightly brush the microwave turntable with oil and arrange the griddlecakes along the edge. Microwave for 6 minutes on 100 per cent power (high). Brown the griddlecakes over the coals until brown on both sides.

Makes 12 griddlecakes.

Tested in a 600-watt oven.

Easy microwaved health rusks

Hannetjie Niemand of Touws River uses 2-litre ice-cream containers to make these rusks in the microwave oven. We tried out the recipe in the test kitchen, with excellent results.

- 375 ml (1½ c) brown sugar
- 500 g margarine
- 2 extra-large eggs
- 1 container (500 ml) buttermilk
- 1 kg self-raising flour
- 15 ml (1 T) baking powder
- 2 ml (½ t) salt
- 750 ml (3 c) All Bran Flakes
- 500 ml (2 c) bran
- 200 ml (⅘ c) sunflower seeds
- 100 ml (⅖ c) raisins
- 500 ml (2 c) wheat germ (optional)

Spray three 2-litre ice-cream containers with nonstick spray.

Place the brown sugar and margarine in a microwave-proof dish. Microwave for 3 minutes on 100 per cent power (high). Stir well and microwave again for 2 minutes.

Beat the eggs and buttermilk together and mix in the margarine mixture.

Combine the rest of the ingredients and add to the margarine mixture. Mix well and turn into the three ice-cream containers. Place on an upturned saucer in the microwave oven and microwave one container at a time for 14-15 minutes on 70 per cent power (medium high). Cool slightly before turning out onto a wire rack to cool completely. Break into pieces and place on a baking sheet. Dry the rusks in a conventional oven at 100 °C (200 °F). Store in airtight containers.

Makes about 65 rusks.

Tested in a 600-watt oven.

Easy microwaved bran rusks

This quick and easy recipe for deliciously crunchy bran rusks was sent in by Mrs Joan Smit of Lynnwood Ridge.

- 500 g self-raising flour
- 500 ml (2 c) bran
- 5 ml (1 t) baking powder
- 5 ml (1 t) salt
- 200-250 g margarine
- 3 extra-large eggs
- 150 ml (⅗ c) brown sugar
- 400 ml (1⅗) buttermilk

Spray two 25 x 12 x 8-cm microwave-proof loaf tins with nonstick spray and line with paper towelling.

Combine the self-raising flour, bran, baking powder and salt. Rub in the margarine with your fingertips until the mixture resembles breadcrumbs.

Beat the remaining ingredients together and blend with the dry ingredients. Mix and turn into the prepared tins. Microwave one tin at a time, placing it on an upturned saucer. Microwave for 9-10 minutes on 50 per cent power (medium). Leave for 10 minutes before turning out on a wire rack.

Cool completely before cutting into fingers. Dry out in a conventional oven at 100 °C (200 °F) until the rusks are completely dry.

Store in an airtight container.

Makes about 50 rusks.

Tested in a 600-watt oven.

Microwaved aniseed rusks

Watching rusks baking in a microwave oven is quite an experience, writes Marlene, who unfortunately forgot to include her surname and address. This recipe is not as time-consuming as it looks, she says. Marlene uses the same mixture to make a raisin loaf.

- about 3 kg cake flour
- 15 ml (1 T) salt
- 2 packets (10 g each) instant yeast
- 25 ml (5 t) aniseed
- 750 ml (3 c) sugar
- 5 eggs, beaten
- 1 can (397 g) condensed milk
- 5 condensed milk cans lukewarm water
- 450 g butter, grated

Spray one or more 22 x 11 x 8-cm microwave-proof loaf tins with nonstick spray. (If you have a longer dish that fits in the microwave oven, use that instead.)

Sift the cake flour and salt together. Add the instant yeast, aniseed and sugar and mix well.

Beat the eggs, condensed milk and lukewarm water together. Add to the dry ingredients and mix well. Knead until the dough no longer sticks to your hands. (Add more cake flour if the mixture is too slack.) Cover with greased plastic wrap and leave the dough to rest in a warm place for 20 minutes.

Knead in the grated butter until the dough no longer sticks to your hands.

Cover once more and leave to rest in a warm place for about 1 hour or until the dough has risen nicely. Do not knock back. Pinch pieces of dough from the dough mass and shape into balls the size of tennis balls. Pack eight balls tightly together in the prepared loaf tin.

Microwave for 1 minute on 100 per cent power (high) to activate the yeast. Leave until the rusks have risen nicely and nearly fill the tin.

Microwave one tin at a time 5-6 minutes uncovered on 100 per cent power (high). Leave for about 5 minutes before turning out. Break into balls and divide each ball into four parts while still slightly warm.

Arrange the rusks on baking sheets and dry in a conventional oven at 100 °C (200 °F). Store in airtight containers.

Makes about 150 rusks.

Tested in a 700-watt oven.

Easy microwaved bran rusks

Microwaved jams

Easy microwaved apricot jam

This recipe, sent in by Mrs Francina van der Merwe of Bloemfontein, is definitely worth making. We tested it in the microwave oven but it can just as easily be made on a conventional stove.

- 1,5 kg apricots (not too ripe)
- 1,5 kg sugar
- 150 ml (⅗ c) water
- 2 ml (½ t) salt
- 30 ml (2 T) lemon juice

Rinse the apricots and cut out all blemishes. Cut in half and remove the stones.

Place alternating layers of apricots and sugar in a large microwave-proof glass bowl. Add the water and salt. Microwave for 10 minutes on 100 per cent power. Stir frequently with a wooden spoon to ensure that all the sugar has dissolved before the mixture comes to the boil.

Add the lemon juice and microwave for 40 minutes on 100 per cent power (high) or until the jam has thickened. Stir well every 10 minutes. Test if the jam is thick enough by dropping a little onto a saucer and cooling it. The jam is ready when it is no longer runny and falls off the spoon in blobs.

Pour into clean sterilised jam jars and seal.

Makes about 800 ml jam.

Tested in a 600-watt oven.

Easy microwaved peach jam

Mrs G. Jordaan of Oudtshoorn was given a present of a large quantity of clingstone peaches. At the same time she invested in a microwave oven, but couldn't find a recipe for peach jam. So she devised this one herself.

- 1 kg clingstone peaches
- 75 ml (5 t) lemon juice
- 500 ml (2 c) sugar
- 12,5 ml (2½ t) margarine

Rinse the peaches well. Peel and slice thinly. (To make a smooth jam, process the peaches in a food processor.)

Place the peaches in a deep 3,5-litre glass bowl. Add the lemon juice and mix well. Cover with cling wrap and microwave for 15 minutes on 100 per cent power (high). Stir every 5 minutes.

Add the sugar and stir well until the sugar has nearly dissolved. Cover and microwave for another 10 minutes on 50 per cent power (medium). Stir every 3 minutes.

Add the margarine and microwave for 20 minutes uncovered on 100 per cent power (high). Stir the jam every 5 minutes.

Pour the jam into sterilised jars and seal.

Makes 500 ml jam.

Tested in a 600-watt oven.

Easy microwaved peach jam

Index

From the microwave oven